BUILDING A SAFETY CULTURE - TRANSFORMING MINDSETS

RACHIT UPADHYAY

To all those who prioritize Safety,

and to the person whom I admire the most

Mr. Chegu Dhanumjaya Sir

Contents

Preface

This book, "Building a Safety Culture - Transforming Mindsets" serves as a comprehensive guide for leaders, employees, and stakeholders who recognize that safety is not merely a regulatory requirement but a fundamental aspect of organizational success. Safety culture is defined as the shared values, beliefs, and practices that prioritize the well-being of individuals in the workplace, creating an environment where safety is woven into the very fabric of everyday operations. It is a culture where employees feel empowered to speak up, where safety is viewed as everyone's responsibility, and where proactive measures are taken to prevent incidents before they occur. The journey to establish such a culture begins with a shift in mindset, a departure from the reactive approaches that often characterize traditional safety practices. Instead of merely responding to incidents, organizations must embrace a proactive, preventive stance that prioritizes safety at all levels—from leadership to frontline workers. This shift requires a deep understanding of human behavior, as culture is ultimately shaped by the actions and attitudes of individuals. Each person in the organization plays a critical role in creating a safe environment, and it is essential to foster a sense of ownership and accountability among all team members. To build a safety culture, leaders must lead by example, demonstrating their commitment to safety through their actions and decisions. This involves not only establishing clear policies and procedures but also engaging in open communication and collaboration. Leaders should create an atmosphere where employees feel comfortable reporting hazards or near misses without fear of repercussions, reinforcing the idea that safety is a shared priority.

In this book, we will explore strategies for effective communication, training, and leadership development, as well as the importance of employee involvement and recognition in fostering a culture of safety. Furthermore, we will discuss the role of continuous improvement and learning in maintaining a safety culture. Organizations must be willing to adapt and evolve, using data and feedback to identify areas for improvement and implement necessary changes. This proactive approach not only enhances safety but also drives overall organizational performance, as a strong safety culture is often linked to increased productivity, employee morale, and retention. As we navigate through the complexities of modern workplaces, the importance of mental health and well-being must also be acknowledged. Whether you are a seasoned safety professional, a leader seeking to instill a culture of safety, or an employee eager to contribute to a safer workplace, this book will provide you with the tools and knowledge necessary to effect meaningful change. By investing in safety, we invest in the well-being of our people, the integrity of our operations, and the success of our organizations. Let this book be your guide as we embark on this vital journey together, transforming mindsets and building a safer, more resilient future for all.

Acknowledgements

To my family and friends, thank you for your support and patience during the countless hours spent in researching and writing this book. Your belief in this project kept me motivated, and your understanding made it possible to pursue this passion.

CHAPTER ONE

NEED FOR SAFETY

In the early stages of industrialization in the 19th century, particularly in Western countries, workplaces were often hazardous, with very few numbers of regulations governing worker safety. The rise of factories led to numerous accidents and health issues, prompting public concern and the first movements advocating for safer conditions. The effective enforcement of The Factory Act in 1830s in United Kingdom aimed to regulate working hours and improve safety standards, marking early legislative efforts to protect workers. Similarly, in the United States, the establishment of labour unions in the late 19th century played a pivotal role in advocating for safer working environments. The formation of American Federation of Labor (AFL) in 1886 highlighted the need for collective bargaining over safety issues. As the safety movement gained momentum globally, several key events catalysed change.

The Triangle Shirtwaist Factory fire in March 1911 in New York City claimed the lives of 146 workers as fire spread on the 8th, 9[th,] and 10th floors in the building. Many of whom were young women recently arrived from Europe, had little time or opportunity to escape. The building had only one fire escape, which collapsed during the rescue effort. Long tables and bulky machines trapped many of the victims. This tragedy galvanized public opinion and led to significant reforms in workplace safety laws, including improved fire safety codes and better working conditions.

In India, the safety movement began to take shape in the early 20th century, particularly during the colonial era when industrialization started to take root. Workers in textile mills and other industries faced dangerous conditions, and the lack of regulatory oversight led to frequent accidents. The first major legislative effort to address workplace safety came with the Factories Act of 1881, which aimed to regulate labour conditions in factories. However, it was limited in scope and implementation.

The International Labour Organization (ILO), founded in 1919, played a crucial role in promoting global labour standards and advocating for worker safety. Through various conventions and recommendations, the ILO has influenced National policies and helped shape the safety movement worldwide.

Post-independence, the Indian government recognized the importance of worker safety and health, enacting the Factories Act of 1948, which provided a comprehensive framework for regulating safety, health, and welfare in factories. This legislation was influenced by international labour standards and aimed to enhance working conditions across various industries. Additionally, the establishment of the Employees' State Insurance Corporation (ESIC) in 1948 marked a significant step toward providing health insurance and social security to workers.

The late 20th century brought increased awareness of occupational health issues, particularly related to emerging technologies and industrial processes. The Bhopal gas tragedy in 1984, one of the worst industrial disasters in history, highlighted the consequences of neglecting safety standards and regulations in India. This incident prompted significant changes in The Factories Act 1948 and the establishment of the Environment Protection Act in 1986 and more stringent regulations on hazardous substances. In recent years, the safety movement has continued to evolve, with a focus on mental health, ergonomic safety etc.

The legal frameworks in the workplace exist to ensure that organizations uphold specific safety standards and practices, creating environments that minimize risks and hazards. In many countries, legislation such as the Occupational Safety and Health Act (OSHA) in the United States and similar regulations in other jurisdictions mandates that employers provide a safe working environment. These laws outline the responsibilities of employers to assess workplace hazards, implement necessary safety measures, and maintain compliance with established safety standards. Failure to adhere to these legal obligations can result in severe consequences, including heavy fines, legal liability, and reputational damage. Organizations are required to take proactive measures to prevent accidents, injuries, and illness that could arise from unsafe working conditions. This includes regular risk assessments, providing adequate training, ensuring the availability of personal protective equipment (PPE), and fostering a culture of safety where employees feel empowered to report hazards without fear of retaliation.

The legal implications of neglecting safety standards can be significant. In the event of workplace accidents or health issues, employers may face lawsuits from injured employees or their families, leading to substantial financial losses and operational disruptions. Additionally, regulatory agencies may conduct investigations following incidents, resulting in penalties and enforcement actions against non-compliant organizations. The existence of safety regulations encourages organizations to adopt best practices, invest in training programs, and continually evaluate their safety procedures to align with legal requirements. Various industry standards and guidelines established by organizations such as the International Organization for Standardization (ISO) and the National Fire Protection Association (NFPA) provide a comprehensive framework for organizations to develop and implement effective safety management systems, ensuring compliance with legal requirements while promoting best practices in safety. Companies are increasingly held accountable not only for their financial performance but also for their ethical practices, including the health and safety of their workforce. Organizations that prioritize safety and comply with legal obligations enhance their reputation, build trust with stakeholders, and demonstrate a commitment to the well-being of employees.

Emerging issues, such as mental health, ergonomic safety, and the impact of remote work, are prompting regulators to update existing laws and introduce new regulations that address contemporary safety challenges. This dynamic environment emphasizes the importance of staying informed about legal requirements and adapting safety practices accordingly. By prioritizing safety, companies can mitigate legal risks, enhance employee morale, and foster a culture of continuous improvement that ultimately leads to a safer and more productive work environment.

The costs related to workplace incidents can be staggering, encompassing medical expenses, legal fees, compensation claims, and potential fines from regulatory agencies. For instance, companies may face increased insurance premiums following accidents, which can drain financial resources and affect profitability. Moreover, workplace injuries often lead to lost man-days, resulting in reduced productivity and increased overtime costs as employers strive to cover for injured employees. From an economic perspective, organizations that prioritize safety tend to enjoy enhanced employee morale and retention. A safe working environment fosters job satisfaction which translates into higher employee retention rates and reduced training costs. Lower employee retention can disrupt operations, further impacting productivity. When employees feel valued and safe, they are more likely to be engaged and committed to their work, driving better performance and innovation.

A strong safety record can serve as a competitive advantage in attracting top talent, as many job seekers prioritize workplace safety when considering employment opportunities. Organizations that invest in safety programs often see long-term benefits through improved reputation and brand loyalty. A commitment to safety can enhance a company's image, making it more appealing to customers, investors, and partners. In many industries, a solid safety track record can differentiate a company from its competitors, leading to increased market share and customer trust.

Safety compliance can be a key factor in securing contracts and business partnerships, especially in sectors where safety standards are rigorously enforced. Companies with robust safety management are often viewed as reliable and responsible, which can lead to greater business opportunities and increased profitability. Non-compliance with safety regulations can result in severe penalties, including fines and sanctions that can significantly impact a company's profit.

Litigation resulting from workplace injuries can lead to costly settlements and damage awards, further straining financial resources. By investing in proactive safety measures, organizations can not only avoid these potential costs but also cultivate a culture of safety that promotes operational excellence. In this regard, the economic benefits of safety extend to enhancing overall organizational resilience. Companies that prioritize safety are better equipped to handle unforeseen challenges, whether they be accidents, regulatory changes, or shifts in market dynamics. This resilience is essential for sustaining operations and maintaining profitability in an increasingly competitive landscape.

The humanitarian perspective emphasizes the intrinsic value of every individual and the right to work in an environment free from harm, injury, or psychological distress. It becomes particularly crucial in industries where workers are exposed to hazardous conditions, such as construction, manufacturing, and healthcare. Ensuring safety is not just about preventing physical injuries, it encompasses the psychological and emotional well-being of employees as well.

A safe workplace fosters a culture of respect and care, where individuals feel valued and secure. This sense of safety contributes to overall mental health, reducing stress and anxiety associated with the fear of accidents or unsafe conditions. When employees believe that their well-being is prioritized, they are more likely to engage fully with their work, leading to improved morale and productivity.

The requirement for safety in humanitarian circumstances extends beyond the immediate workforce to the broader community and society at large. Unsafe working conditions can have far-reaching consequences, affecting families and local economies. For example, when workers are injured on the job, their families may face financial hardships due to lost wages and increased medical expenses. This cascading effect emphasizes the interconnectedness of workplace safety and community health. Organizations that prioritize safety contribute to the overall welfare of their communities by preventing accidents and fostering a culture of responsibility and care. Additionally, the humanitarian viewpoint on safety emphasizes the importance of inclusivity and accessibility. All employees, regardless of their background or abilities, have the right to work in a safe environment.

Safety initiatives aligns closely with corporate social responsibility (CSR) initiatives, where organizations recognize their role in contributing positively to society. Companies that actively engage in promoting safety not only enhance their reputation but also demonstrate a commitment to ethical practices that extend beyond profit-making.

By investing in safety training, equipment, and programs, organizations send a powerful message about their values and priorities. This commitment to safety can foster goodwill among stakeholders, including customers, employees, and community members, reinforcing the idea that business success is intertwined with social responsibility.

In the global context, the need for safety is increasingly recognized as a fundamental human right. International Labour Organization (ILO), advocate for safe and healthy working conditions as essential components of human dignity and development. By promoting safety standards worldwide, these organizations aim to eliminate exploitation and unsafe practices that compromise workers' rights and well-being. Ultimately, prioritizing the safety is about fostering a culture that values human life, dignity, and well-being. Organizations that embrace this perspective are not only fulfilling their ethical obligations but are also creating environments where individuals can thrive. This commitment to safety enhances employee satisfaction, strengthens community ties, and contributes to a more equitable society.

CHAPTER TWO

Challenges in Building a Safety Culture

As regulatory landscapes evolve, often in response to new research, technological advancements, or emerging industry practices, safety professionals must remain vigilant and proactive to adapt their policies and procedures accordingly. The pace at which regulations change can create a whirlwind of pressure on organization. Each regulatory update necessitates a detailed analysis of existing safety procedures to determine whether adjustments are needed, and this can become overwhelming, particularly for organizations that are already understaffed or under-resourced. The sheer volume of regulations that organizations must monitor can be staggering, especially in industries with stringent oversight, such as construction, healthcare, and manufacturing.

The challenge of maintaining compliance is further complicated by the fact that regulations can vary significantly between jurisdictions. For organizations operating in multiple locations, the safety department must grapple with the complexities of differing state and local regulations, which can lead to confusion and inconsistency in safety practices across the organization. Employees in different locations may find themselves subjected to varying safety procedures, which can not only create potential legal liabilities but also lead to frustrations among the workforce. A lack of uniformity in safety practices can undermine the overall safety culture, as employees may perceive some locations as being less safe than others, leading to a divided commitment to safety.

The consequences of non-compliance can be severe, ranging from financial penalties to increased scrutiny from regulatory bodies and reputational damage. Organizations that fail to adhere to safety regulations may face costly fines, which can significantly impact their finances. Moreover, incidents arising from non-compliance can result in workplace injuries, legal liabilities, and even criminal charges in severe cases, all of which can have far-reaching implications for the organization. This creates an environment where organizations must not only prioritize compliance but also cultivate a culture of accountability, ensuring that all employees understand their roles and responsibilities regarding safety.

The lack of long-term commitment to safety by management within an organization also poses a significant challenge in establishing and maintaining a robust safety culture. When leadership fails to prioritize safety as a core organizational value, it often results in short-lived initiatives that lack the necessary resources and attention to create lasting change. This lack of commitment can manifest in various ways, such as infrequent safety training, insufficient funding for safety programs, and the absence of ongoing assessments of safety practices. Management may implement safety measures only in response to incidents or regulatory pressures, leading employees to perceive safety as a reactive rather than proactive endeavour. When safety is not viewed as a long-term priority, the organizational narrative shifts toward production and profitability, sidelining the importance of a safe working environment. This creates a culture where safety concerns are often ignored or downplayed, as employees may fear that sharing such concerns could jeopardize their standing in the company or disrupt production flow.

The lack of long-term commitment from management can lead to a disconnect between safety policies and everyday practices. Employees may receive initial training, but without ongoing reinforcement and updates, their understanding of safety procedures can diminish over time. This gap in knowledge can result in unsafe behaviours, as employees may revert to old habits or overlook important safety measures that are no longer actively promoted. Moreover, the absence of sustained leadership involvement in safety initiatives can hinder the effectiveness of safety programs. When management is not visibly engaged, it sends a message that safety is not a priority, leading to a lack of accountability at all levels. Employees may be less likely to take ownership of their safety responsibilities when they see that their leaders are not fully invested in promoting a safe work environment.

The effectiveness of establishing and maintaining safety standards can be severely undermined by lack of authority and support from senior management. It generates into a scenario where safety officers find themselves in a frustrating position, unable to enforce safety measures or make crucial decisions independently. When organizations do not empower safety officers with the authority to implement and enforce safety procedures, the responsibility for safety becomes diluted, leading to a culture where safety is deprioritized. This situation can result in dire consequences, including increased workplace accidents, injuries, and even fatalities.

The effectiveness of safety professionals hinges on their ability to advocate for and implement safety measures, but when they lack the necessary backing from management, their recommendations may fall on deaf ears. For instance, a safety officer may identify a significant risk in the workplace and propose the implementation of new safety equipment or training programs. However, if management is unwilling to allocate the necessary resources or prioritize these recommendations, the safety officer's efforts become futile. This disconnect between the safety officer's expertise and management's decisions creates a challenging environment where safety is often viewed as a liability, overshadowed by production and profit motives.

The lack of authority can lead to a culture of complacency among employees. When workers see that safety measures are not being enforced or taken seriously by management, they may feel justified in disregarding safety procedures themselves. This attitude can result in unsafe behaviour, such as neglecting to wear personal protective equipment (PPE) or bypassing safety procedures to meet production demands. Over time, this environment can foster a perception that safety is not a priority within the organization, which can have cascading effects on overall employee morale and engagement. Employees may become disengaged, feeling that their safety is not valued.

When safety officers do not have the authority to enforce policies, it can create a significant gap in communication regarding safety issues. Safety officers often rely on data collected from incident reports, safety audits, and employee feedback to identify hazards and recommend improvements. However, if they lack the power to act on these findings or if their recommendations are routinely ignored, the organization misses out on valuable opportunities for learning and improvement. In this context, incidents may go unreported or unresolved, preventing the organization from learning from past mistakes and improving safety practices. The situation becomes even more critical in high-risk industries, such as construction or manufacturing, where the consequences of inadequate safety measures can be catastrophic. Without the support of senior management, safety officers may struggle to foster a culture of accountability and transparency, where employees feel empowered to report hazards and adhere to safety procedures.

Another significant challenge is the habitual practices. Employees may resist change or view safety procedures as unnecessary, especially if they have been working in a certain way for a long time. This resistance is often rooted in a combination of psychological and cultural factors that contribute to a reluctance to adapt to new practices, even if those practices are designed to enhance safety. When individuals have developed routines and methods over time, they tend to find comfort and familiarity in these established processes. This comfort can lead to a mindset that views any alteration as a potential disruption, causing anxiety about the unknowns associated with new procedures.

Employees may perceive changes to safety procedures as a challenge to their competence or ability, especially if they believe that their longstanding practices have served them well. This sense of threat can lead to defensive behaviour, where employees dismiss the need for new safety measures, arguing that the previous methods have not resulted in incidents or injuries. The way changes are communicated plays a crucial role in shaping employee perceptions. If management fails to effectively articulate the reason behind new safety procedure, employees may struggle to understand their importance and relevance. In instances where employees feel that they have not been adequately consulted or involved in the decision-making process, their resistance can intensify. When workers perceive that safety measures are imposed upon them without their input, they may develop a feeling that their expertise and experience are undervalued. This disconnect can create an adversarial relationship between employees and management, further hindering the successful adoption of new safety procedures.

Employees may also resist change due to the fear of increased workload or additional responsibilities. New safety procedures often come with new training requirements, documentation, or procedural changes that may be perceived as cumbersome or time-consuming. When employees are already balancing multiple tasks and deadlines, the prospect of incorporating additional safety measures into their routines can feel overwhelming. This perception can lead to a tendency to resist changes, particularly if employees believe that the new procedure will complicate their work without delivering clear benefits.

Peer influence can play a significant role in shaping attitudes toward safety. If employees observe their colleagues resisting change or dismissing new safety measures, they may be more likely to adopt a similar stance. This social reinforcement of resistance can create a culture where non-compliance becomes normalized, making it even more challenging for management to effect meaningful change.

Insufficient budget can also significantly hinder organization's ability to implement safety initiatives effectively, creating a cascading effect that impacts overall workplace safety and employee well-being. When budgets are tight, organizations often find themselves prioritizing compliance over comprehensive safety strategies. This can lead to a reactive approach, where the focus shifts to merely meeting regulatory requirements rather than fostering a proactive safety culture. Limited funding restricts the ability to invest in essential safety training, equipment, and technology that can mitigate risks. Without adequate resources, safety professionals may struggle to conduct thorough risk assessments or implement necessary safety procedures, leaving employees vulnerable to hazards.

Insufficient staff means that safety officers are often handling multiple responsibilities that dilute their effectiveness. This can lead to missed inspections, inadequate safety training sessions, and a lack of follow-up on safety incidents, ultimately compromising the integrity of safety programs.

When safety staff are overburdened, they may not have the time or capacity to engage with employees, which is crucial for building trust and fostering a culture of safety. Employee participation is essential for identifying potential hazards and encouraging reporting of near misses, but when safety staff are under-resourced, the lines of communication may weaken. This lack of engagement can result in a workforce that feels disconnected from safety initiatives, which can further erode safety culture.

Insufficient budget constraints may limit the ability to adopt new technologies that could enhance safety measures, such as advanced monitoring systems or safety management software. These tools can streamline reporting and data analysis, providing insights that inform better decision-making and resource allocation. When an organization fails to allocate sufficient funds to its safety department, it not only jeopardizes the immediate safety of its employees but also risks incurring long-term costs associated with workplace injuries, increased insurance premiums, and potential legal liabilities. The inability to properly address safety concerns can lead to higher accident rates, which ultimately impact productivity and morale.

Employees who witness or experience unsafe conditions may become disengaged, leading to a workforce that is less motivated and more likely to overlook safety procedures. Employees may receive training that does not resonate with their specific experiences or hazards. This can result in gaps in knowledge and an overall lack of preparedness to handle safety challenges. The impact of underfunding in safety departments can also extend to employee morale and retention. Workers are more likely to feel valued and engaged in a workplace that prioritizes their safety. When employees perceive that their safety is not a priority often due to inadequate resources and staff they may seek employment elsewhere, leading to lower retention rates that can further strain the safety. Lower retention rate means constantly onboarding new employees who may require extensive training, consuming additional resources and time.

When organizations fail to demonstrate a commitment to safety through adequate funding, they may struggle to attract top talent, as prospective employees increasingly prioritize workplace safety when evaluating job opportunities. The cumulative effect of these challenges can severely undermine an organization's reputation and competitiveness. In industries where safety is paramount, such as construction or manufacturing, a reputation for poor safety practices can deter clients, investors, and potential employees alike. This can have long-lasting implications for business viability and growth.

Frequent changes in processes within an industry can significantly impact safety, often leading to increased risks and hazards in the workplace. One of the primary consequences of these changes is that employees may struggle to keep up with the new procedures and requirements, leading to confusion and potential lapses in safety practices. If training on updated processes is not thorough or consistent, workers might not fully understand the safety implications of the changes, resulting in unsafe behaviour and increased vulnerability to accidents.

Frequent process changes can disrupt established safety routines and habits. Employees who have become accustomed to specific safety measures may find it challenging to adjust to new procedures, particularly if these changes are implemented without sufficient explanation or justification. This disruption can foster a culture of complacency, where employees believe that their prior knowledge is adequate despite the new processes.

The lack of adequate communication regarding changes can lead to misunderstandings and misinterpretations of safety guidelines, further increasing the risk of incidents. When employees are uncertain about the latest procedures or the motive behind them, they may hesitate to ask questions or seek clarification, creating a gap in knowledge that can have serious consequences. When workers are preoccupied with adapting to new processes, their focus on safety may diminish, heightening the risk of accidents. The mental load associated with frequent changes can result in fatigue and reduced attention to detail, critical factors in maintaining a safe work environment. Organizations may struggle to implement effective safety monitoring and evaluation systems amidst continuous changes.

The lack of proper safety equipments in an organization can significantly compromise workplace safety, leading to increased risks for employees and potentially devastating consequences for the organization. When safety equipment is inadequate, outdated, or unavailable, employees are left vulnerable to workplace hazards, which can result in injuries, illnesses, and even fatalities. For instance, in high-risk environments such as construction sites or manufacturing facilities, the absence of appropriate personal protective equipment (PPE) like helmets, gloves, goggles, and aprons can expose workers to serious dangers, including falls, chemical exposures, and machinery-related injuries. This not only affects the immediate well-being of employees but also impacts overall morale and productivity. Employees who feel unsafe or unprotected are likely to experience increased anxiety and stress, which can lead to decreased job satisfaction.

The lack of safety equipment can lead to a culture of negligence, where employees may feel compelled to take shortcuts or ignore safety procedures simply to keep up with production demands. When safety equipment is not prioritized, it sends a clear message to employees that their safety is not valued by the organization. Regulatory compliance becomes a significant issue when safety equipment is lacking. Organizations that fail to provide the necessary safety gear can face legal penalties, increased insurance premiums, and lawsuits from injured employees. Regulatory bodies often require strict adherence to safety standards, and non-compliance can lead to severe financial consequences.

The limited visibility of safety within an organization often undermines the effectiveness of safety programs and initiatives. When safety is not visibly prioritized by leadership, it can create a perception among employees that safety is merely a checkbox exercise rather than a fundamental organizational value. This invisibility manifests in several ways, including inadequate communication about safety policies, infrequent safety training sessions, and a general absence of safety-related discussions in everyday operations. Employees may feel uncertain about the importance of safety procedures, leading to inconsistent adherence to established practices. when incidents do occur, they may not be thoroughly investigated or communicated to the broader workforce, preventing valuable lessons from being learned and applied in the future. Consequently, employees might perceive that reporting unsafe conditions or incidents is futile, further discouraging open dialogue about safety issues. This lack of visibility can create an environment where safety becomes an afterthought, rather than an integral component of daily operations.

Organizations often struggle with a lack of standardized metrics to measure safety performance, which compounds the issue of invisibility. Without clear indicators of safety performance, it becomes challenging to identify trends, celebrate successes, or address deficiencies effectively. Employees may not see the tangible impact of their safety efforts, leading to disengagement and a lack of motivation to prioritize safety in their work.

Identifying safety hazards and accurately assessing risks within an organization requires thorough knowledge that combines expertise, experience, and ongoing education. Safety hazards can take many forms, including physical, chemical, ergonomic, and psychosocial risks, and recognizing them demands a keen understanding of the specific work environment, the tasks being performed, and the potential dangers associated with those tasks. For instance, in a manufacturing setting, safety professionals must be well-versed in the machinery used, the materials handled, and the processes in place to identify potential hazards effectively. This involves not only understanding the equipment and materials but also being aware of how they interact with each other and the environment. Knowledge of industry regulations and standards is equally crucial. Safety professionals must stay updated on changes in regulations and best practices to ensure that their hazard assessments are accurate and current.

Thorough knowledge of risk assessment methodologies is essential. Various techniques, such as the Hierarchy of Controls, FMEA (Failure Mode and Effects Analysis), Why - Why Analysis and JHA (Job Hazard Analysis), can be employed to evaluate risks systematically. Understanding these methodologies allows safety professionals to prioritize risks and determine the most effective strategies for mitigation.

Employees not reporting incidents and near misses due to fear of reprisal is also a significant challenge in many industries. When employees hesitate to come forward with information about safety issues or near misses, it creates a dangerous environment where risks go unaddressed and accidents become more likely. This fear of negative consequences can stem from a variety of factors, including a workplace culture that punishes mistakes, a lack of trust in management, and the perception that reporting will not lead to meaningful change. In many cases, employees may have witnessed colleagues facing disciplinary actions for incidents that were beyond their control. Such experiences can foster a culture of silence, where individuals prioritize self-preservation over safety communication. In these settings, the repercussions of not reporting can be severe, potentially leading to injuries or fatalities that could have been prevented through proactive measures.

The absence of incident reporting hampers organizations' ability to learn from mistakes. Each near miss or incident contains valuable lessons that can inform safety practices and prevent future occurrences. When employees feel that they cannot report these events without facing retaliation, the organization loses out on crucial insights that could enhance safety procedures and training programs. Without accurate reporting, safety officers find it difficult to identify trends or address systemic issues that contribute to unsafe conditions.

The fear of reprisal often extends beyond disciplinary actions. Employees may also worry about social repercussions, such as damage to their reputation among colleagues. In a competitive workplace, where individuals are vying for promotions or recognition, the thought of being perceived as a "whistleblower" can deter employees from speaking up. This social pressure can create an environment where individuals feel isolated, leading to increased stress and anxiety about their job security and relationships with peers. As a result, employees may choose to downplay incidents or ignore safety procedures altogether, further increasing the risk of accidents.

CHAPTER THREE

Role of Leadership in Safety

Leadership plays a pivotal role in establishing and nurturing a safety culture within an organization, fundamentally shaping how safety is perceived and practiced among employees. The tone set by leaders directly influences the attitude and behaviour of the workforce regarding safety procedures and practices. When leaders prioritize safety, it communicates to employees that their well-being is a top concern, fostering an environment where safety is not merely a compliance requirement but a core value.

One of the primary ways leaders set this tone is through their actions. Employees observe their leaders closely, and if they see management actively engaging in safety practices such as participating in safety training, conducting regular safety inspections, and adhering to safety procedures they are more likely to adopt similar behaviour. This role modelling is essential when leaders visibly prioritizes safety. It signals to the entire organization that safety matters, creating a culture where safe behaviour is the norm.

Effective communication is another critical component of leadership that shapes safety culture. Leaders must articulate the importance of safety in a clear and consistent manner, not just through policies but also by sharing the reasoning behind safety measures. By explaining the reasons for safety principles and discussing potential consequences of neglect, leaders can foster a deeper understanding and appreciation for safety among employees. Proper communication channels encourage employees to share their concerns and suggestions, creating a collaborative atmosphere where safety is seen as a shared responsibility. Recognition and accountability also play vital roles in cultivating a safety-oriented culture.

When leaders recognize and reward safe behaviour, it reinforces the notion that safety is valued within the organization. This recognition can take various forms, from informal praise to formal awards and celebrations of safety milestones. Such practices boost morale and encourage employees to engage in safe practices actively. Accountability is also crucial. Leaders must consistently enforce safety procedures and rules and address unsafe actions. By doing so, they demonstrate that safety is non-negotiable and that everyone, regardless of their position, is responsible for maintaining a safe workplace.

Leaders can influence safety culture by investing in training and development. Comprehensive safety training programs equip employees with the necessary knowledge and skills to perform their jobs safely while signalling the organization's commitment to safety. Leaders who prioritize ongoing training emphasize that safety is an evolving practice requiring continuous learning and improvement.

Cultivating psychological safety is essential for a robust safety culture. Employees need to feel safe to speak up about safety concerns without fear of retaliation. Leaders can foster this environment by encouraging open discussions about safety issues and ensuring that employees know their voices will be heard and valued. When employees believe they can report near misses or unsafe conditions without negative consequences, they are more likely to engage in proactive safety behaviour, contributing to a culture of continuous improvement. Leadership is fundamental in setting the tone for safety culture within organizations.

This strong safety culture not only protects employees but also enhances overall organizational performance, resulting in improved safety outcomes and a healthier workplace for all. Ultimately, a committed leadership approach to safety culture sets the stage for sustainable success and well-being in the workplace.

Leading Safety: Management's commitment to a secure workplace - First and foremost, management must establish a clear safety policy that outlines the organization's commitment to safety and health. The policy should articulate the company's safety goals, responsibilities, and the importance of safety in achieving overall organizational success. This policy should be regularly reviewed and updated to reflect changes in regulations, technology, and workplace practices.

Management must ensure that all employees receive comprehensive training on safety procedures, equipment usage, and emergency response procedures. This training should be tailored to specific roles within the organization, providing employees with the knowledge and skills needed to identify hazards and respond appropriately. Regular refresher courses and drills can reinforce this training, helping to keep safety practices at the forefront of employees' minds.

Another critical aspect of management's role is conducting thorough risk assessments and audits. Identifying potential hazards and evaluating their impact on workers is fundamental to preventing accidents and injuries. Management should facilitate regular inspections of the workplace, involving employees in the process to gain insights from those who are directly engaged in operations.

In addition to identifying risks, management must also implement effective safety measures and controls. This includes providing appropriate personal protective equipment (PPE), ensuring machinery is maintained and operated safely, and establishing clear procedures for handling hazardous materials. Management should also allocate sufficient resources for safety initiatives, demonstrating a commitment to creating a safe working environment.

Management plays a pivotal role in incident investigation and analysis. When accidents or near-misses occur, it is essential to conduct thorough investigations to determine root causes and prevent recurrence. This involves analysing the circumstances surrounding the incident, gathering input from involved persons, and identifying any systemic failures that may have contributed to the event.

Management should communicate findings transparently and implement corrective actions to address identified weaknesses. Promoting a culture of safety also requires management to lead by example. Leadership should demonstrate safe behaviour, comply with safety procedures, and actively participate in safety initiatives. When employees observe management prioritizing safety, they are more likely to adopt similar attitudes and practices. Recognizing and rewarding safe behaviour can further reinforce this culture, encouraging employees to take ownership of their safety and that of their colleagues.

Safety First: Excellence through effective management systems - A good safety management system integrates policies, procedures, practices, and resources aimed at ensuring a safe working environment for employees, thereby minimizing the likelihood of accidents, and promoting overall organizational efficiency. A clear safety policy that articulates the organization's commitment to maintaining high safety standards is the core of safety management system. This policy serves as the foundation for all safety initiatives and should be communicated to all employees, outlining the roles and responsibilities of both management and staff.

Risk assessment involving regularly identifying and evaluating potential hazards associated with processes, equipment, and work environments is also a part of it. This proactive approach allows organizations to implement risk management strategies designed to eliminate or mitigate identified risks. Employees must receive thorough training on safety procedures, emergency response procedures, and the correct use of personal protective equipment (PPE).

Communication plays a key role in the success of a safety management system. Organizations should establish clear channels for sharing safety information, such as regular safety meetings and updates, to keep all employees informed about safety policies, procedures, and any changes that may occur.

Documentation is equally important. Maintaining comprehensive records of safety policies, training sessions, incident reports, and risk assessments ensures accountability and provides a basis for continuous improvement. A robust safety management system also includes mechanisms for incident reporting and investigation. When accidents or near misses occur, prompt reporting encourages transparency and enables timely corrective actions. Investigations should focus on identifying root causes rather than assigning blame, allowing organizations to learn from incidents and implement preventive measures effectively.

Performance monitoring is another critical aspect. Organizations should establish key performance indicators (KPIs) to track safety metrics such as incident rates, compliance with training programs, and the completion of risk assessments. Safety should not be viewed as a standalone function but rather as an integral part of the organizational strategy.

Aligning Goals, Achieving Success: Management by Objective - MBO plays a crucial role by aligning safety objectives with overall business goals, fostering a culture of safety, and ensuring active participation from all levels of the organization. It is a strategic management model that focuses on setting specific, measurable goals enhancing organizational effectiveness and accountability. The process begins with senior management defining clear safety objectives that align with the organization's vision and mission. These objectives should be specific, measurable, achievable, relevant, and time-bound (SMART), ensuring clarity and focus. For instance, an organization might set a goal to reduce workplace incidents by a certain percentage within a specified timeframe. Once these overarching objectives are established, they are communicated throughout the organization, encouraging all employees to understand their role in achieving safety goals. This communication fosters a sense of ownership and accountability, as employees can see how their contributions directly impact safety outcomes.

In MBO, individual performance is linked to these safety objectives, creating a framework where employees are evaluated based on their ability to meet safety-related goals. This approach not only motivates employees to prioritize safety in their daily tasks but also emphasizes the importance of personal responsibility in maintaining a safe working environment. Regular progress reviews are integral to the MBO process, allowing management to assess the effectiveness of safety initiatives and make necessary adjustments. These reviews provide opportunities for feedback and discussion, enabling employees to share concerns and insights on safety practices. This collaborative approach not only enhances employee engagement but also promotes continuous improvement in safety policies and practices.

MBO encourages the establishment of safety performance indicators, which are essential for measuring progress toward safety goals. These indicators might include metrics such as incident rates, training completion rates, and compliance with safety procedures. By tracking these metrics, organizations can identify trends, recognize areas for improvement, and celebrate achievements in safety performance. The data gathered through these indicators can inform future safety policy formulations.

MBO promotes cross-department collaboration. When safety objectives are integrated into the overall business strategy, various departments can work together to identify shared goals and develop comprehensive safety initiatives. For example, the maintenance department might collaborate with operations to ensure that equipment is regularly inspected and that safety practices are consistently followed. This collaborative effort helps in fostering a unified approach to safety that engages all employees.

Another significant aspect of MBO is its focus on training and development. To achieve safety objectives, organizations must invest in employee training programs that enhance safety awareness and skills. MBO encourages the identification of training needs based on safety goals, ensuring that employees are equipped with the necessary knowledge to adhere to safety procedures. By aligning safety goals with overall business objectives, promoting employee engagement, and establishing measurable performance indicators, MBO creates a proactive safety culture that prioritizes continuous improvement.

Guardians of Safety: Ensuring a Safe Workplace - Safety department serves as the backbone of an organization's safety management system, tasked with developing, implementing, and overseeing safety policies and procedures tailored to the specific risks associated with the industry. One of the primary functions of the safety department is to conduct comprehensive risk assessments to identify potential hazards in the workplace.

By systematically analysing processes, equipment, and environments, safety professionals can evaluate risks and prioritize them based on their potential impact on employees and operations. This proactive approach enables the organization to implement effective control measures to mitigate identified risks before they result in incidents or injuries. Training and education are also fundamental responsibilities of the safety department.

The department is responsible for designing and delivering safety training programs that equip employees with the necessary knowledge and skills to recognize hazards and respond appropriately. These training sessions cover a wide range of topics, including the proper use of personal protective equipment (PPE), emergency response procedures, and specific safety procedures related to the industry. Regular training not only ensures compliance with regulatory requirements but also fosters a culture where safety is valued and prioritized by all employees.

Safety department plays a crucial role in monitoring compliance with government safety regulations. This involves staying informed about relevant industry standards, as well as conducting regular audits and inspections to ensure that safety procedures are being followed. When non-compliances are identified, the safety department is responsible for developing corrective action plans and working with management to implement necessary changes.

Incident Reporting and Investigation are other vital functions of the safety department. When accidents or near-misses occur, the department facilitates thorough investigations to determine root causes and contributing factors. This process not only helps to address the immediate issues but also provides valuable insights that can lead to long-term improvements in safety practices. By analysing trends in incidents and identifying common risk factors, the safety department can develop targeted interventions to prevent future occurrences.

Communication is another key aspect of the safety department's role. Safety Department serves as a central hub for sharing safety information throughout the organization. Regular safety meetings and updates ensure that all employees are informed about current safety policies, procedures, and any changes that may arise. The department also encourages communication channels, allowing employees to report safety concerns or suggest improvements without fear of retaliation.

Safety department collaborates with other departments to integrate safety considerations into everyday operations. By working closely with engineering, production, maintenance and human resources, the safety department ensures that safety is embedded into the organizational culture and that all employees understand their roles in maintaining a safe work environment.

The safety department also engages in continuous improvement efforts, regularly reviewing and updating safety policies and practices to adapt to new challenges, technologies, and regulatory changes. This commitment to continuous improvement not only enhances workplace safety but also fosters employee morale and productivity, as workers feel valued and protected.

By fulfilling these responsibilities, the safety department contributes significantly to creating a safe working environment, ultimately enhancing the overall performance and success of the organization. Through its efforts, the department not only protects employees but also supports the organization's goals and objectives by minimizing disruptions caused by accidents and injuries.

Measure Safety, Maximize Protection: Performance Monitoring for a Safer Workplace - Effective safety performance monitoring begins with the establishment of key performance indicators (KPIs) that serve as measurable benchmark for safety outcomes. Common KPIs may include incident rates, near-miss reports, employee training completion rates, and compliance with safety procedures. By collecting and analysing data related to these indicators, organizations can gain valuable insights into their safety performance and identify areas needing improvement.

Regular audits and inspections are integral to this monitoring process. Safety audits involve comprehensive evaluations of workplace practices, equipment, and compliance with established safety standards. These audits help to identify hazards, assess risk management strategies, and ensure that safety procedures are being followed. Through proactive identification of potential risks, organizations can take corrective actions before accidents occur, thereby enhancing overall safety.

Another vital aspect of safety performance monitoring is incident reporting and analysis. When accidents or near misses occur, thorough investigations are essential to understand the root causes and contributing factors. This process not only addresses immediate safety concerns but also allows organizations to learn from incidents, ultimately preventing recurrence. By analysing patterns in incidents, organizations can develop targeted interventions, such as additional training or changes in processes, to mitigate identified risks. Employee involvement is also crucial in safety performance monitoring. This involvement fosters a sense of ownership and responsibility among employees, creating a more proactive safety culture. Regular safety meetings and feedback sessions can enhance communication between management and employees, ensuring that safety concerns are promptly addressed and that employees feel empowered to contribute to safety initiatives.

The use of technology plays an increasingly important role in safety performance monitoring. Advanced tools such as data analytics, software for tracking incidents, and mobile applications for reporting hazards can streamline the monitoring process and provide real-time insights into safety performance. These technologies facilitate data collection, analysis, and reporting, allowing organizations to respond quickly to emerging safety issues.

As regulations, industry standards, and workplace conditions evolve, organizations must adapt their safety programs accordingly. Regular reviews ensure that safety practices remain effective and relevant, helping organizations to stay ahead of potential risks. Management commitment to safety performance monitoring is essential. Leaders must prioritize safety as a core organizational value, allocating resources for monitoring activities and supporting continuous improvement efforts. This commitment not only enhances safety practices but also builds trust and accountability within the workforce.

Empowering Safety: Data-Driven Decisions for a Safer Workplace - A Management Information System (MIS) in industrial safety plays a crucial role in enhancing the effectiveness and efficiency of safety management practices within organizations. By systematically collecting, processing, and analysing safety-related data, MIS provides valuable insights that inform decision-making and promote a proactive safety culture. An effective MIS integrates various components such as data collection, analysis, reporting, and communication, all aimed at improving safety outcomes.

The data collected can include incident reports, near-miss occurrences, employee safety training records, safety audits, and compliance with regulatory standards. By centralizing this information, organizations can maintain an up-to-date repository that facilitates easy access and analysis.

One of the primary advantages of utilizing an MIS in industrial safety is its ability to identify trends and patterns in safety performance. For instance, by analysing incident data over time, safety managers can pinpoint recurring issues, such as specific types of accidents or areas with higher incident rates. This trend analysis enables organizations to prioritize safety initiatives and allocate resources effectively to address the most pressing safety concerns.

MIS enhances communication within the organization regarding safety practices and policies. By providing real-time data and dashboards, it allows for timely access of safety information to employees and management. This transparency fosters a culture of accountability and encourages employees to engage in safe practices, knowing that their actions are being monitored and evaluated. Many industries are subject to stringent safety regulations that require detailed record-keeping and reporting. An effective MIS can automate these processes, generating necessary reports and documentation efficiently, thereby reducing the administrative burden on safety officer. This automation not only ensures compliance but also allows safety officers to focus on strategic initiatives rather than getting bogged down in paperwork. Training and development are other critical areas where an MIS can make a significant impact. By tracking employee training records and identifying gaps in safety knowledge, organizations can tailor training programs to meet specific needs. For instance, if data reveals that a particular department is struggling with safety compliance, targeted training sessions can be implemented to address those deficiencies. This targeted approach not only enhances employee competency but also contributes to overall safety performance.

MIS supports incident investigation and root cause analysis by providing structured frameworks for analysing safety incidents. By collecting relevant data and facilitating collaboration among various departments, an MIS helps teams to conduct thorough investigations and identify underlying causes of accidents. This analytical capability allows organizations to implement corrective actions, thereby preventing similar incidents in the future.

In addition, the integration of technology such as mobile applications and wearable devices into an MIS can further enhance industrial safety. Employees can report hazards in real time, access safety procedures, and receive alerts regarding potential risks through these technological tools. This immediate access to information empowers employees to take proactive measures to ensure their safety and that of their colleagues.

Management Information System in industrial safety is indispensable for promoting a culture of safety and ensuring compliance with regulations. By providing a centralized platform for data collection, analysis, and reporting, MIS enables organizations to make informed decisions, identify trends, and allocate resources effectively. Through the effective implementation of an MIS, organizations can significantly enhance their safety performance, ensuring the well-being of their workforce while achieving operational excellence.

Crafting Safety Trainings: Design and Development - The assessment of need, design, and development of a safety training program in industry is a vital process that ensures employees are equipped with the knowledge and skills necessary to maintain a safe work environment and adhere to industry regulations.

The initial phase involves a comprehensive evaluation of the current safety practices, identifying gaps in knowledge, skills, and compliance among employees. This can be achieved through a variety of methods, including safety audits, employee surveys, incident reports, and consultations with safety officers and managers. By analysing historical data on workplace accidents and near misses, organizations can pinpoint specific areas where training is necessary, such as proper equipment usage, emergency procedures, or hazard recognition.

Gathering input from employees about their experiences and perceived training is crucial, as it helps in creating a more effective training program that addresses the real challenges faced in the workplace. Once the assessment phase is complete, the next step is the design of the safety training program. This involves setting clear, measurable objectives that align with both the organizational safety goals and the identified trainings. For instance, objectives might include ensuring all employees are trained in the use of personal protective equipment (PPE) by a given deadline.

The design phase should also consider the learning styles of participants, incorporating a variety of instructional methods such as interactive workshops, simulations, hands-on training, and e-learning modules to cater to diverse learning preferences. Engaging training materials that include visual aids, real-life scenarios, and case studies can enhance understanding and retention, making the training more impactful. Following the design phase, the development of the safety training program takes center stage. This involves creating the actual content, which may include developing training manuals, presentations, instructional videos, and assessment tools. It is crucial to ensure that all materials are not only informative but also relevant to the specific roles and environments in which employees operate.

Selecting qualified trainers or facilitators who possess both technical knowledge and effective teaching skills is essential for delivering the training effectively. Pilot testing the program with a small group of employees can provide valuable feedback on the content and delivery methods, allowing for adjustments before a full-scale rollout.

After implementing the training program, the evaluation of its effectiveness is paramount. This can be done through a combination of pre- and post-training assessments to measure knowledge gain of safety practices in the workplace. Gathering feedback from participants regarding the training experience can also provide insights into its relevance and effectiveness. This evaluation phase is critical for continuous improvement.

Organizations should regularly review and update the training program based on new safety regulations, emerging hazards, and evolving industry standards. By fostering a culture of continuous learning and adaptation, organizations can ensure that their safety training programs remain effective and relevant.

Safety Starts with Strategy: Train Smart, Stay Safe - Safety training methods and strategies in industries are essential for equipping employees with the necessary skills and knowledge to maintain a safe work environment. A variety of training methods can be employed to engage employees effectively, ensuring that safety procedures are understood and adhered to. One common method is classroom training, where instructors deliver information through lectures, presentations, and discussions. This approach is particularly useful for imparting theoretical knowledge about safety regulations, hazard recognition, and emergency procedures. However, to enhance retention and engagement, it is often beneficial to supplement classroom training with interactive elements such as quizzes or group discussions.

Another effective strategy is hands-on training, which allows employees to practice safety procedures in a controlled environment. This method is particularly crucial for industries that involve the use of machinery or equipment. For example, workers can be trained on operating heavy machinery or using personal protective equipment (PPE) through practical demonstrations and simulations, ensuring that they can apply their knowledge in real-world situations. On-the-job training (OJT) is another valuable approach, where employees receive guidance from experienced colleagues while performing their tasks. This method facilitates immediate feedback and reinforcement of safety practices, allowing employees to learn in the context of their specific roles.

E-learning has gained popularity in recent years, especially with the advent of digital technologies. Online training modules and courses provide flexibility, allowing employees to learn at their own pace and revisit materials as needed. E-learning can incorporate multimedia elements such as videos, interactive scenarios, and assessments, making it an engaging option for many learners.

Organizations can use virtual reality (VR) and augmented reality (AR) technologies to create immersive training experiences. These technologies enable employees to experience realistic simulations of hazardous situations, helping them develop critical decision-making skills without the risks associated with actual hazards. Safety drills and simulations are also vital components of effective training strategies. Regularly scheduled drills, such as fire evacuations or emergency response exercises, ensure that employees are familiar with safety procedures and can act swiftly in real emergencies. These drills can help identify weaknesses in emergency procedures and provide opportunities for improvement.

Peer-led training encourages a culture of safety by involving employees in the training process. When employees train their peers, it fosters open communication and trust, making it easier to discuss safety concerns and best practices. This collaborative approach can enhance the relevance of training, as employees may feel more comfortable asking questions and sharing insights in a familiar environment. Another key strategy involves continuous safety education, where training is not viewed as a one-time event but rather an ongoing process.

Regular refresher courses, safety meetings, and updates on new regulations or technologies keep safety at the forefront of employees' minds and reinforce a culture of safety. Organizations can also leverage safety performance metrics to identify training needs and assess the effectiveness of their safety programs. By analysing data on incidents, near misses, and compliance rates, organizations can tailor their training efforts to address specific gaps in knowledge or behaviour. Emphasizing a collaborative and adaptable training approach not only enhances safety outcomes but also fosters a culture of proactive engagement in safety practices.

Evaluate to Elevate: Review, Refine, Reinforce Safety - Evaluation and review of safety training programs are critical components in ensuring their effectiveness and relevance within an organization. This process begins with setting clear evaluation criteria based on the training objectives established during the program's design phase. These criteria often include knowledge retention, behavioral changes, and improvements in safety performance metrics, such as incident rates and near misses. A robust evaluation framework typically employs various assessment tools to gauge the effectiveness of the training.

One of the most common methods is pre- and post-training assessments, which measure participants' knowledge before the training and their understanding afterward. These assessments provide quantitative data on how much knowledge has been gained and help identify any areas where additional training may be needed. Additionally, conducting surveys or feedback forms after training sessions can offer qualitative insights into participants' perceptions of the training. Questions regarding the clarity of the material, the effectiveness of the training methods used, and the overall engagement level can highlight strengths and areas for improvement.

On-the-job performance evaluations play a vital role in assessing the practical application of skills learned during training. Supervisors can observe employees in their work environment to determine if they are implementing the safety procedures correctly and adhering to best practices. This observational feedback is invaluable, as it not only reinforces training concepts but also identifies gaps in knowledge or compliance that may require further training.

Another essential aspect of evaluation involves analysing safety performance metrics over time. Organizations should track data related to workplace incidents, injuries, and compliance with safety procedures before and after the implementation of the training program. A noticeable reduction in incidents can be a strong indicator of the training's effectiveness.

Regular safety audits can help organizations assess whether the training has led to changes in behaviour and workplace culture. Continuous improvement is a fundamental principle in evaluating safety training programs. Organizations should establish a regular review cycle to assess the training program's content, delivery methods, and overall effectiveness. This review process should consider any changes in regulations, industry standards, and emerging safety trends that may necessitate updates to the training material. Engaging employees in the evaluation process is also beneficial. Their feedback can provide insights into the training's practicality and relevance to their daily tasks. Incorporating employee suggestions can lead to the development of more targeted and engaging training programs, ultimately enhancing safety outcomes.

Benchmarking against industry standards and best practices can help organizations identify gaps in their training programs and adopt innovative strategies to enhance effectiveness. Collaborating with safety professionals and participating in industry safety forums can provide valuable insights into effective training methodologies and emerging safety practices. The evaluation and review of safety training programs are essential for ensuring that these initiatives are not only effective but also continuously evolving to meet the needs of the organization and its workforce.

Ultimately, organizations that prioritize the evaluation of their safety training programs demonstrate a proactive approach to risk management and employee well-being, leading to improved safety performance and reduced workplace incidents.

Promoting Safety: Building a Safer Workplace - Safety promotional activities in the industry play a crucial role in fostering a culture of safety and ensuring the well-being of employees. These initiatives encompass a wide range of strategies designed to raise awareness about safety procedures, reduce workplace accidents, and enhance overall safety performance. One of the most effective methods is distribution of informative materials such as brochures, posters, and safety bulletins, which serve as constant reminders of safe practices and potential hazards. Regular training programs that educate employees on safe work practices, emergency procedures, and the proper use of personal protective equipment (PPE) is also beneficial. These training sessions not only provide essential knowledge but also empower employees to take an active role in their own safety and that of their colleagues.

Organizing safety contests can motivate employees to engage more actively in safety initiatives. By rewarding individuals or teams who demonstrate exceptional safety practices, companies can create a competitive spirit that encourages everyone to prioritize safety. This approach not only boosts morale but also reinforces the importance of adhering to safety standards.

Regular safety meetings and open forums where employees can discuss safety concerns and share suggestions are vital components of a successful safety promotional strategy. These meetings foster a sense of community and collective responsibility, allowing employees to share their opinions and contribute to safety improvements. Another critical aspect of safety promotion is the use of technology, such as safety apps or digital platforms, which can streamline communication and provide real-time updates on safety issues. By utilizing these tools, companies can ensure that all employees, regardless of their location, have access to the latest safety information and resources.

Conducting safety audits and inspections not only helps identify potential hazards but also demonstrates the organization's commitment to maintaining a safe working environment. Sharing the results of these audits with employees can promote transparency and encourage a proactive approach to safety. Collaborating with external safety organizations or experts can also enhance an organization's safety initiatives. Partnering with these entities can provide access to additional resources, training, and certifications, elevating the overall safety standards within the industry.

Another effective strategy is to celebrate safety milestones, such as achieving a certain number of days without accidents. Acknowledging these achievements publicly can reinforce the importance of safety and motivate employees to maintain high standards. Integrating safety into the company's core values and mission statement can ensure that it remains a priority at all levels of the organization. Ultimately, safety promotional activities should be ongoing and adaptable to the evolving nature of the workplace and industry standards.

Investing in Safety Today for a Safer Tomorrow - A safety budget in the industrial sector is a critical component that reflects an organization's commitment to maintaining a safe working environment. Allocating funds specifically for safety initiatives ensures that companies can effectively implement measures designed to prevent workplace accidents and injuries. This budget typically covers various aspects, including employee training, personal protective equipment (PPE), safety audits, and maintenance of safety equipment. Investing in comprehensive training programs is essential, as it equips employees with the knowledge and skills needed to recognize hazards and respond appropriately in emergencies. By allocating budget for activities like regular safety drills and workshops, organizations can foster a culture of safety awareness, ensuring that all employees, from new hires to experienced persons, remain vigilant and informed about best practices.

A portion of the safety budget should be earmarked for the purchase of high-quality PPE. This includes helmets, gloves, goggles, and other necessary equipment designed for specific hazardous jobs. Ensuring that employees have access to the right protective gear not only complies with regulatory requirements but also significantly reduces the likelihood of injuries on the job.

Regular maintenance and replacement of safety equipment, such as fire extinguishers, safety harnesses, and first aid kits, are also essential expenses within the safety budget. By ensuring that these items are in good working condition, companies can enhance their emergency preparedness and response capabilities. By allocating funds for regular audits, organizations can take proactive steps to address issues before they lead to accidents, ultimately saving costs related to workplace injuries, insurance claims, and lost productivity.

Safety budget should also be consider in implementing safety management software or technology solutions that streamline safety reporting, incident tracking, and compliance monitoring. Investing in such technology can provide valuable insights into safety performance metrics, enabling companies to make data-driven decisions and continuously improve their safety practices. Engaging employees in safety initiatives is paramount, and this can be facilitated through safety committees or other Out-Bound Trainings. Allocating funds for employee involvement initiatives, such as safety contests, recognition programs, or incentive schemes, can boost morale and encourage a collective commitment to safety. These activities not only foster a sense of ownership among employees but also reinforce the importance of safety as a shared responsibility.

By viewing safety as an investment rather than a cost, organizations can cultivate a robust safety culture that not only protects employees but also enhances overall productivity and operational efficiency. A well-planned safety budget ultimately pays dividends in the form of reduced incidents, lower insurance premiums, and improved employee morale, demonstrating that prioritizing safety is both a sound business strategy and a moral obligation. In an ever-evolving industrial landscape, maintaining a strong focus on safety through strategic budgeting is essential for long-term success and sustainability.

Safety Starts with Smart Planning - Planning for Safety is a cornerstone of any successful industrial operation, ensuring that workplaces are not only compliant with regulations but also genuinely protective of employee well-being.

This process begins with a thorough risk assessment, which identifies potential hazards within the workplace, evaluates their severity, and determines the likelihood of incidents occurring. By understanding these risks, organizations can prioritize their safety initiatives and allocate resources effectively. Once the hazards are identified, the next step involves developing a comprehensive safety plan that outlines clear policies and procedures drafted to mitigate those risks. This plan should include specific guidelines for emergency response, incident reporting, and communication procedures, ensuring that all employees are aware of their roles in maintaining a safe environment.

Training is another critical component of effective safety planning. Regular training sessions equip employees with the necessary knowledge and skills to recognize hazards, respond appropriately to emergencies, and use personal protective equipment (PPE) correctly. Training should be an ongoing process, with refreshers and updates integrated into the schedule to account for new hazards or changes in operations. This commitment to education fosters a culture of safety where employees feel empowered to prioritize their well-being and that of their colleagues.

Engaging employees in the safety planning process is vital. By involving workers in discussions about safety practices and policies, organizations can tap into their insights and experiences, leading to more practical and relatable safety measures. Creating safety committees or other meeting groups that include representatives from various departments can enhance communication and ensure that diverse perspectives are considered in the planning process.

In addition, effective safety planning should incorporate regular safety audits and inspections. These evaluations help organizations identify compliance gaps and areas for improvement, ensuring that safety measures are consistently applied and updated as needed. By setting a schedule for routine audits, companies can maintain a proactive approach to safety, addressing potential issues before they escalate into serious incidents. Furthermore, Technology can significantly enhance safety planning. Safety management software can streamline reporting, incident tracking, and compliance monitoring, providing real-time data that informs decision-making.

By utilizing digital tools, organizations can analyse trends in safety performance, identify recurring issues, and implement targeted interventions. It is crucial to regularly review and update the safety plan to adapt to changing conditions, new regulations, or emerging risks. This ongoing assessment ensures that safety measures remain relevant and effective in addressing current challenges.

Overall, planning for safety is a dynamic and continuous process that requires collaboration, communication, and commitment from everyone in the organization. By prioritizing safety in planning efforts, companies can create a safer working environment, reduce the likelihood of accidents, and enhance overall productivity.

Building Safety Together: Management, Employees, Unions United! - Management plays a crucial role in this process by establishing a framework for safety communication that prioritizes transparency and inclusiveness. Regular safety meetings, briefings, and training sessions are essential for sharing information about safety procedures, recent incidents, and best practices. By encouraging managers to actively engage with employees during these discussions, organizations can cultivate an environment where workers feel comfortable sharing their concerns and suggestions. This two-way communication is fundamental. It allows management to address potential hazards while also providing employees with the opportunity to contribute their insights, which are invaluable given their firsthand experience on the job.

It is essential for management to establish clear channels for reporting safety issues. This can include anonymous reporting mechanisms, which empower employees to speak up without fear of reprisal. A robust reporting system not only helps identify safety concerns but also demonstrates management's commitment to addressing them promptly. Transparency in how reported issues are handled fosters trust and reinforces the belief that employee safety is a top priority.

Regular updates on the status of reported safety concerns can keep employees informed and engaged, highlighting the organization's dedication to their well-being. Involving unions in safety communication is equally important. Unions serve as advocates for workers and can facilitate dialogue between employees and management. Regular meetings between union representatives and management can ensure that safety issues are addressed collaboratively. By including union representatives in safety committees, organizations can leverage their expertise and insights to enhance safety programs. This collaborative approach not only helps in identifying risks but also fosters a sense of ownership among employees, as they see their union actively participating in safety initiatives.

Safety communication should extend beyond formal meetings. Utilizing various communication tools such as newsletters, bulletin boards, and digital platforms can keep safety information accessible and top of mind for employees. Visual reminders like safety posters can effectively communicate key safety messages and rules in a way that is easy to understand. Training programs should also be designed to encourage ongoing communication about safety. For instance, conducting workshops that focus on team-building and safety collaboration can enhance relationships among employees, management, and union representatives, ultimately creating a more cohesive approach to safety.

Regular feedback sessions can also help refine safety procedures and ensure they remain relevant and effective in addressing the evolving challenges in the workplace. Recognizing the contributions of both management and employees in achieving safety goals encourages continuous dialogue and commitment to safety initiatives.

By prioritizing transparency, collaboration, and continuous feedback, organizations can foster a culture where safety is everyone's responsibility. This commitment not only enhances workplace safety but also promotes trust and morale among all stakeholders, leading to a more productive and engaged workforce.

CHAPTER FOUR

HOW MINDSET AFFECTS BEHAVIOUR

Developing a safety mindset is a critical endeavour that involves a sophisticated approach to awareness, behaviour, and culture, ensuring that safety becomes an integral part of daily life, both personally and professionally.

To begin with, cultivating awareness is the cornerstone of a safety mindset. This means consistently assessing your environment for potential hazards, whether at home, work, or in social networks. Take the time to identify risks that may not be immediately obvious. This could include anything from cluttered walkways to the proper use of equipment. Regularly asking yourself questions like, "What could go wrong here?" encourages a proactive approach rather than a reactive one, fostering a mindset that prioritizes prevention.

Education plays a pivotal role in shaping a safety-conscious mindset. Engaging in safety training and workshops equips individuals with the knowledge they need to recognize hazards and respond appropriately. Understanding the principles of risk assessment and emergency procedures instills confidence and reinforces safe practices, creating a foundation upon which a safety culture can be built. It is also essential to create an environment where open communication about safety is encouraged. Fostering a culture that prioritizes discussion about safety concerns allows individuals to share their thoughts without fear of criticism. When everyone feels empowered to share their perspectives on safety, it cultivates a sense of collective responsibility that enhances overall safety practices.

Leading by example is an effective way to instill a safety mindset in others. Demonstrating safe behaviour, whether it's wearing protective gear, adhering to safety procedures, or simply being mindful of your surroundings, sets a standard for others to follow. People are more likely to adopt a safety mindset when they see those around them practicing it consistently.

Another crucial aspect of developing a safety mindset is personal responsibility. Recognizing that safety is not just the responsibility of managers or designated safety officers but everyone's duty encourages individuals to take ownership of their actions. This means making conscious decisions that prioritize safety and understanding the impact of one's behaviour on others. Encouraging a proactive stance involves consistently evaluating personal habits, such as not rushing through tasks or overlooking safety procedures for convenience.

Incorporating regular safety checks into daily routines can reinforce a safety mindset. Whether it's inspecting equipment before use, organizing workspaces to minimize hazards, or conducting regular safety audits, these practices serve as reminders that safety is an ongoing commitment. Mindfulness also plays a critical role in developing a safety mindset. Practicing mindfulness involves being present in the moment and fully aware of your surroundings. This heightened state of awareness can prevent accidents and help individuals respond effectively to unexpected situations. Techniques such as deep breathing, meditation, or simply taking a moment to pause before acting can greatly enhance one's focus and decision-making abilities in potentially risky situations.

Recognizing and rewarding safe behaviour whether through verbal acknowledgment, incentives, or formal recognition programs can motivate individuals to prioritize safety. This not only reinforces the desired behaviour but also fosters an environment where safety is celebrated rather than merely enforced. Embracing a mindset of continuous improvement is essential in the journey towards safety. This means being open to learning from mistakes and near-misses. Analysing incidents without assigning blame allows for valuable lessons to be extracted, ultimately leading to improved safety procedures and practices. Encouraging a growth mindset, where individuals view challenges and setbacks as opportunities for learning, can greatly enhance safety awareness and practices.

It is vital to adapt safety practices to changing circumstances. Whether it's new technology, updated regulations, or evolving workplace dynamics, being flexible and willing to adjust safety measures ensures that they remain relevant and effective. Embracing innovation in safety practices, such as utilizing new safety equipment or software, can also lead to enhanced protection and a stronger safety culture. Looking to the future, it's important to stay informed about emerging trends and technologies in safety. Proactively seeking out information on best practices and advancements can position individuals and organizations to maintain a strong safety mindset.

Awareness is Action: Don't Just See, Observe! - Cultivating situational awareness is a crucial skill that enhances safety and decision-making in everyday life. It involves being acutely aware of your surroundings, understanding the context of your environment, and recognizing potential hazards or changes that could impact your safety or the safety of others.

The first step in developing situational awareness is to cultivate a mindset of observation. This means actively engaging with your environment rather than passively moving through it. Practice scanning your surroundings regularly, taking note of machines, equipments, objects, and any potential risks. This could include identifying exits in a crowded space, recognizing unusual behaviour, or being aware of environmental conditions that could pose a danger, such as wet floors or poorly lit areas. It is essential to be mindful of not just what you see, but also what you hear and feel. Sounds can indicate potential hazards, like machinery operating in a dangerous manner or the approach of an emergency vehicle. Likewise, paying attention to changes in the atmosphere, such as sudden silence in a noisy area, can alert you to something wrong.

Developing situational awareness also involves understanding the context of the environment you are in. This includes recognizing the norms and behaviour typical to that work area. Regularly assessing your environment fosters a habit of proactive thinking. Instead of reacting to situations as they arise, you begin to anticipate potential problems before they escalate. This anticipatory mindset can significantly reduce the likelihood of accidents or conflicts. Practicing mindfulness techniques can enhance your ability to remain present and attentive. Simple exercises like deep breathing or momentarily pausing to take in your surroundings can sharpen your focus and improve your overall awareness.

Another valuable tool for cultivating situational awareness is the use of checklists or mental prompts. Before entering a new environment, mentally run through a checklist of things to observe: exits, potential hazards, and the behaviour of those around you. This structured approach helps ensure that nothing goes unnoticed and reinforces the habit of being observant.

Sharing this practice with others can create a culture of situational awareness. In your work area, encourage colleagues to share their observations and concerns, fostering an environment where everyone feels responsible for safety. This collaborative approach not only enhances individual awareness but also builds a collective understanding of the environment, leading to improved safety outcomes. Regularly reflecting on your experiences can further develop your situational awareness.

After encountering various situations, take time to evaluate what went well, what could have been improved, and how your awareness influenced the outcome. This reflection reinforces learning and helps identify patterns that enhance your ability to assess situations effectively in the future. Cultivating situational awareness is an ongoing process that requires practice and commitment. By prioritizing observation, understanding context, and actively engaging with your environment, you develop a heightened sense of awareness that not only enhances personal safety but also contributes to the safety and well-being of those around you.

Safe Actions, Great Rewards! - Rewarding safe behaviour is a powerful strategy for encouraging a mindset change toward safety in both personal and professional environments. When individuals are recognized and rewarded for their commitment to safe practices, it reinforces the idea that safety is not merely a set of rules to follow but a fundamental value that benefits everyone.

One of the most effective ways to implement this strategy is through positive reinforcement. This can take many forms, from verbal acknowledgment and praise to tangible rewards such as gift cards, water bottle, tea cups or other recognition items. The key is to ensure that the rewards are meaningful to the individuals being recognized, as this will enhance motivation and encourage ongoing safe behaviour. Creating a culture that celebrates safety requires consistent communication about the importance of safe practices and the impact they have on overall well-being.

Regularly highlighting examples of safe behaviour within the organization or community can serve as inspiration for others, demonstrating that safety is a shared responsibility and that each individual's actions contribute to a larger goal. This can be accomplished through safety meetings, mail communications or social media posts that spotlight individuals or teams who exemplify safe practices.

Implementing formal recognition programs can institutionalize the practice of rewarding safe behaviour. For instance, organizations can establish monthly or quarterly awards for employees who consistently demonstrate a commitment to safety, creating a competitive yet supportive environment where everyone strives to contribute to a safer workplace. Such programs not only motivate individuals but also promote teamwork, as peers often encourage each other to adopt safe practices to be eligible for recognition.

Involving employees in the creation and implementation of these programs can enhance buy-in and ensure that the rewards align with what they value. Encouraging feedback about what types of recognition would be most meaningful can lead to a more engaged workforce that feels genuinely appreciated for their efforts. Beyond formal recognition, fostering an environment where safety is discussed openly and positively reinforces the importance of safe behaviour.

Creating forums or platforms where individuals can share their safety experiences, successes, and challenges fosters a sense of community and collective responsibility. This open dialogue can lead to the sharing of best practices and innovative safety solutions, further reinforcing the importance of safety as a shared value.

It is also important to recognize that rewarding safe behaviour is most effective when it is part of a broader safety culture that includes education, training, and open communication. Safety training should emphasize the importance of safe practices and the potential consequences of unsafe behaviour, allowing individuals to connect their actions with tangible outcomes. When individuals understand the "why" behind safety procedures, they are more likely to internalize these practices as part of their daily routines.

As environments evolve, so too should the criteria for recognition to ensure they remain relevant and motivating. Ultimately, rewarding safe behaviour is a crucial component of developing a robust safety mindset. This not only leads to enhanced safety practices but also cultivates an environment where individuals feel valued and empowered to contribute to the well-being of themselves and those around them.

Employee Engagement and Empowerment

Fostering a sense of ownership and accountability in safety is crucial for creating a proactive safety culture within an organization. When employees feel personally responsible for safety, they are more likely to engage in safe practices and contribute to a culture where safety is prioritized. One effective strategy is to involve employees in the development and implementation of safety policies and procedures. When workers have their inputs in shaping safety procedures and rules, they are more likely to understand and appreciate the purpose behind them, leading to increased commitment. Conducting workshops or safety committees where employees can express their ideas and concerns encourages collaboration and demonstrates that their input is valued.

Another key strategy is to provide comprehensive training that emphasizes the importance of individual roles in maintaining safety. Training should not only cover the technical aspects of safety procedures but also highlight the consequences of unsafe behaviour, reinforcing the notion that every employee plays a vital role in the overall safety of the workplace. By fostering an environment of continuous learning, organizations can help employees recognize the importance of their contributions to safety.

Recognizing and rewarding safe behaviour can significantly enhance feelings of ownership and accountability. When employees are acknowledged for their commitment to safety whether through verbal praise, safety awards, or incentive programs, it reinforces positive behaviour and encourages others to adopt the same behaviour. Creating a recognition program that celebrates safety milestones can further motivate employees to take ownership of their safety practices.

Regular feedback is also essential for fostering accountability. Leaders should engage in ongoing discussions about safety performance and encourage employees to share their observations and experiences. This two-way communication not only helps identify areas for improvement but also empowers employees to take responsibility for their safety and that of their peers.

Implementing a transparent incident reporting system is another strategy that can cultivate a sense of ownership. When employees feel safe to report near misses or unsafe conditions without fear of retaliation, they are more likely to engage in proactive safety behaviour. It is crucial to frame incident reporting as a learning opportunity rather than a blame mechanism, emphasizing that every report contributes to the overall improvement of safety practices.

Setting clear expectations for safety performance is vital. Organizations should establish specific safety goals and performance metrics that are communicated to all employees. By outlining what accountability looks like in terms of safety, employees can better understand their responsibilities and the importance of meeting these expectations. Regularly reviewing safety metrics and discussing them during team meetings reinforces the idea that safety is a collective responsibility.

Promoting a culture of teamwork and collaboration enhances the sense of ownership in safety. Encouraging employees to look out for one another and take collective responsibility fosters an environment where safety is viewed as a shared value. Team-building activities centred around safety can help strengthen relationships and enhance communication, making it easier for employees to support each other in maintaining a safe workplace.

By implementing these strategies, organizations can create an environment where employees feel empowered to take responsibility for their safety and that of their colleagues, ultimately leading to a stronger safety culture and improved safety outcomes.

Safety Committees: Where Every Voice Counts! - Worker participation in safety management is an essential element of creating a safe and healthy workplace. When employees are actively involved in safety initiatives, the likelihood of accidents and injuries diminishes significantly. This collaborative approach not only enhances the effectiveness of safety procedures but also fosters a culture of safety where every individual feels a sense of ownership and responsibility. One of the key benefits of worker participation is that employees bring unique insights and experiences to the table. They are often the first to identify potential hazards in their specific work environments and can provide valuable feedback on existing safety practices.

By encouraging open communication, organizations can tap into this wealth of knowledge, leading to more practical and effective safety solutions. Incorporating worker participation begins with establishing clear channels for communication. Regular safety meetings, open forums, and suggestion boxes can serve as platforms for employees to share their concerns, share ideas, and report unsafe conditions. Management should actively encourage this dialogue by demonstrating that employee input is valued and taken seriously. A culture of transparency not only builds trust but also motivates employees to engage more fully in safety initiatives.

Involving employees in the development and review of safety policies, procedures, rules can ensure that these guidelines are relevant and effective. When workers participate in crafting safety procedures, they are more likely to understand and adhere to them, as they have had a hand in shaping the rules that govern their work environment.

Training is another critical aspect of promoting worker participation in safety management. Comprehensive training programs should not only cover safety procedures and rules but also emphasize the importance of active involvement in safety initiatives. By equipping employees with the skills and knowledge they need to identify hazards and respond appropriately, organizations empower them to take an active role in their own safety as well as that of their colleagues. Ongoing training sessions can serve as a platform for sharing updates on safety practices and gathering feedback from employees on their experiences and challenges.

Safety committees that include representatives from various levels of the organization can be an effective way to formalize worker participation. These committees provide a structured environment where employees can contribute to safety discussions, identify issues, and propose solutions. By ensuring that a diverse group of employees is represented, organizations can benefit from a broader range of perspectives and ideas. Regular meetings of safety committees can facilitate ongoing dialogue between management and employees, ensuring that safety remains a top priority.

Recognition and rewards for safety participation can further motivate employees to engage in safety initiatives. Implementing programs that celebrate individuals or teams for their contributions to safety can foster a positive safety culture. This recognition not only boosts morale but also reinforces the idea that safety is a shared responsibility. When employees see that their efforts are acknowledged and appreciated, they are more likely to continue participating actively in safety management.

Another effective strategy for enhancing worker participation is to involve employees in incident investigations. When accidents or near misses occur, having workers participate in the investigation process allows them to gain insights into the underlying causes of these incidents. This participatory approach not only helps identify corrective actions but also promotes a culture of learning rather than blame. Employees are more likely to take safety seriously when they see that their input is valued in addressing and preventing future incidents.

Technology can play a significant role in facilitating worker participation in safety management. Utilizing digital platforms for safety reporting and feedback can streamline communication and make it easier for employees to share their concerns and suggestions. Mobile apps and online portals can provide real-time access to safety information, enabling workers to report hazards or unsafe conditions instantly.

By harnessing technology, organizations can create a more inclusive environment where all employees feel empowered to contribute to safety efforts. Involving workers in safety management also aligns with regulatory requirements and industry best practices. Many safety regulations emphasize the importance of employee participation in creating and maintaining safe workplaces. By actively engaging employees, organizations not only comply with these requirements but also demonstrate a genuine commitment to safety. This proactive approach can lead to improved safety performance and reduced incidents, ultimately benefiting the organization as a whole.

Fostering worker participation in safety management can have positive implications for overall organizational culture. When employees feel that their inputs are heard and valued, job satisfaction and morale increase. A strong safety culture, characterized by open communication and collaboration, can lead to higher levels of employee engagement and productivity. When workers take ownership of safety, they are more likely to look out for one another, creating a supportive and cohesive work environment. As organizations continue to evolve and face new challenges, prioritizing worker participation in safety management will be crucial for ensuring the health and safety of all employees.

Motivation Matters: Transforming Safety Culture Through Theory! - Understanding safety motivation is crucial for developing effective safety management systems in any organization. Theories of safety motivation help explain why individuals prioritize safety behaviour and how various factors influence their commitment to workplace safety. These theories can be categorized into several frameworks, each offering unique insights into the dynamics of motivation and behaviour in relation to safety.

Behavioral theories focus on the observable actions of individuals and the environmental factors that reinforce or discourage these actions. The most prominent theory in this category is B.F. Skinner's Operant Conditioning. According to this theory, in a safety context, positive reinforcement such as rewards for safe behaviour can motivate employees to adhere to safety practices. Conversely, if unsafe behaviour leads to negative consequences, employees are likely to avoid such actions in the future. This approach emphasizes the importance of establishing clear safety policies and consistent enforcement, where safe behaviour is recognized and unsafe behaviour is addressed.

Cognitive theories explore the mental processes behind decision-making and behaviour. One well-known cognitive theory related to safety is the Theory of Planned Behaviour (TPB) proposed by Ajzen. This theory posits that an individual's intention to perform a behaviour is influenced by three factors: attitudes toward the behaviour, subjective norms, and perceived behavioral control. In the context of safety, if employees believe that safety behaviour lead to positive outcomes (attitude), feel that their peers and supervisors expect them to follow safety practices (subjective norms), and believe they have the ability to perform that behaviour (perceived behavioural control), they are more likely to engage in safe practices. Thus, fostering a positive attitude toward safety, establishing supportive social norms, and enhancing employees' confidence in their ability to follow safety procedures can significantly impact safety motivation.

Albert Bandura's Social Learning Theory emphasizes the role of observation and imitation in learning behaviour. According to this theory, individuals can learn safety behaviour by observing others, especially role models or peers who demonstrate safe practices. This theory highlights the importance of mentoring and peer influence in promoting safety. When employees see their colleagues adhering to safety procedures, they are more likely to emulate that behaviour. Organizations can harness this theory by creating opportunities for employees to witness safe practices, such as through training sessions, safety demonstrations, or job shadowing programs. Cultivating a strong safety culture where employees openly share experiences and learn from each other can enhance safety motivation.

Maslow's Hierarchy of Needs offers another perspective on safety motivation. This psychological theory proposes that individuals are motivated by a hierarchy of needs, starting from basic physiological needs to higher-order psychological needs. In the workplace, safety is often linked to the fulfilment of physiological and safety needs. Employees must feel secure in their environment before they can focus on higher-level needs, such as belonging, esteem, and self-actualization. Organizations that prioritize safety create a foundation for employees to feel secure, allowing them to engage more fully in their work and pursue professional growth. Ensuring that employees have the necessary safety equipment, training, and resources addresses their fundamental safety needs, thereby enhancing overall motivation.

Herzberg's Two-Factor Theory, also known as the Motivation-Hygiene Theory, distinguishes between hygiene factors and motivators. Hygiene factors, such as salary, job security, and working conditions, can lead to dissatisfaction if they are inadequate. In contrast, motivators such as recognition, responsibility, and opportunities for growth can enhance job satisfaction and motivation. In terms of safety, organizations must address hygiene factors by ensuring that safety conditions are adequate and compliant with regulations. Once hygiene factors are met, they can focus on motivators, such as recognizing employees for safe behaviour and providing opportunities for involvement in safety initiatives. This dual approach can foster a motivated workforce that values safety.

Safety Climate Theory examines how employees' perceptions of safety policies, procedures, and practices within an organization influence their motivation to engage in safe behaviour. A positive safety climate, characterized by visible management commitment to safety, clear communication of safety expectations, and a supportive environment, fosters a culture where employees feel motivated to prioritize safety. Conversely, a negative safety climate can lead to complacency and disregard for safety practices. Organizations can assess their safety climate through surveys and feedback mechanisms, using the results to identify areas for improvement and enhance safety motivation.

Self-Determination Theory (SDT) focuses on intrinsic and extrinsic motivations. According to SDT, individuals are more motivated when they feel autonomous, competent, and related to others. In the safety context, fostering intrinsic motivation where employees engage in safe practices because they value safety can lead to more sustainable safety behaviour. Organizations can promote autonomy by involving employees in safety decision-making, allowing them to contribute to safety initiatives. Enhancing competence through training and skill development empowers employees to feel confident in their safety practices. Building a sense of relatedness through teamwork and collaboration further strengthens motivation to adhere to safety procedures.

Expectancy Theory assumes that individuals are motivated to act based on their expectations of the outcomes of their actions. This theory comprises three components: expectancy (belief that effort will lead to performance), instrumentality (belief that performance will lead to rewards), and valence (value placed on the rewards). In safety management, if employees believe that following safety procedures will lead to a safer work environment (expectancy), that adherence will be recognized or rewarded (instrumentality), and that they value those rewards (valence), they are more likely to engage in safe behaviour.

How Perception Shapes Safety - The perception of employees regarding safety in the industry plays a critical role in shaping workplace culture and influencing safety outcomes. Employees' beliefs and attitudes towards safety practices can significantly affect their behaviour and compliance with safety measures, ultimately impacting the overall safety performance of the organization. When employees perceive safety as a priority, they are more likely to engage in safe practices, report hazards, and participate in safety training programs. Conversely, if they view safety measures as mere formalities or a hindrance to productivity, compliance may dwindle, leading to increased risk of accidents and injuries.

Several factors influence how employees perceive safety, including management commitment, workplace culture, and individual experiences. A strong commitment from management is fundamental. When leaders visibly prioritize safety and demonstrate genuine concern for employee well-being, it fosters a culture where safety is valued. Employees are more likely to trust that safety procedures are designed to protect them rather than simply fulfill regulatory requirements.

Effective communication plays a key role here. When management regularly communicates the importance of safety through meetings, training sessions, and visible safety reminders, it reinforces the message that safety is not just a checklist item but an integral part of the organizational ethics. A positive safety culture, characterized by openness, trust, and collaboration, significantly influences employees' perceptions.

In environments where employees feel comfortable discussing safety concerns without fear of reprisal, they are more likely to report unsafe conditions and suggest improvements. This participatory approach enhances engagement and empowers employees to take ownership of their safety. Conversely, a culture of blame or negligence can lead to apathy, where employees disengage from safety practices due to a lack of trust or fear of repercussions.

Individual experiences also shape perceptions of safety. Employees who have experienced or witnessed accidents may become more cautious and aware of safety procedures. Conversely, those who have never encountered safety issues may become complacent, underestimating the importance of adhering to safety measures. Personal backgrounds, including prior safety training and previous workplace experiences, can also influence how individuals approach safety in their current roles.

The role of training in shaping perceptions cannot be overstated. Comprehensive safety training programs not only educate employees about safety procedures but also instill a sense of responsibility towards their own safety and that of their coworkers. When employees understand importance of safety procedures and can see their effectiveness in preventing accidents, their commitment to safety is likely to increase. Incorporating interactive training methods, such as simulations and real-life scenarios, can enhance learning and retention, making safety practices more relatable and memorable.

Recognition and reward systems can further enhance employees' perceptions of safety. When organizations celebrate safety achievements and recognize individuals or teams for their contributions to a safe workplace, it reinforces the idea that safety is valued and that everyone plays a role in maintaining it. This not only motivates employees to comply with safety practices but also fosters a sense of community and shared responsibility.

Also, ongoing feedback mechanisms are essential in shaping employees' perceptions of safety. Regularly soliciting input from employees about safety practices and addressing their concerns demonstrates that management values their opinions and is committed to continuous improvement. When employees see that their feedback leads to tangible changes, it enhances their trust in the organization and reinforces their commitment to safety.

Positive Attitude Lead to Safer Outcomes! - Employees' attitudes towards safety in industries significantly influence workplace dynamics and overall safety performance. These attitudes encompass beliefs, perceptions, and behavioral intentions regarding safety practices, impacting how employees approach their responsibilities and respond to safety procedures.

A positive attitude towards safety fosters compliance with safety measures, encourages proactive behaviour, and creates an environment where employees feel empowered to report hazards and engage in safety discussions. Conversely, negative attitude can lead to complacency, increased risk-taking, and a higher likelihood of accidents.

One primary factor shaping the attitude is the organizational culture. In workplaces where safety is prioritized and integrated into everyday operations, employees are more likely to adopt a proactive stance on safety. When management visibly demonstrates a commitment to safety through regular communication, training, and the allocation of resources, it establishes a positive tone that encourages employees to view safety as a shared responsibility. For instance, regular safety meetings, open forums for discussing safety concerns, and the establishment of clear safety procedures signal to employees that their well-being is valued, reinforcing a collective commitment to safety. Conversely, in organizations where safety is treated as a mere compliance issue or a secondary concern, employees may develop negative attitude. If safety measures are perceived as burdensome or unnecessary, compliance may diminish. Employees might feel that safety procedures hinder productivity or that their feedback is ignored, leading to disengagement and a lack of accountability. This perception can foster a culture where safety is undervalued and where employees do not feel personally invested in safety outcomes.

Training and education also play a critical role in shaping attitude towards safety. Comprehensive safety training equips employees with the knowledge to identify hazards and respond appropriately, reinforcing the importance of safety in their daily tasks. When training is engaging, relevant, and practical, employees are more likely to adopt a positive attitude towards safety. Ongoing training sessions and refreshers can help maintain awareness and combat complacency, ensuring that safety remains a priority over time. Additionally, peer influence significantly affects employees' safety attitude. When colleagues model safe behaviour and prioritize safety, it creates a positive feedback loop, encouraging others to adopt similar practices. Conversely, if unsafe behaviour are normalized within a team, employees may feel pressured to conform, leading to a decline in overall safety attitude. Thus, fostering a collaborative environment where employees support one another in maintaining safety standards is essential.

Recognition and reward systems also contribute to shaping positive attitude towards safety. Acknowledging and rewarding employees' safe practices and contributions to a safer work environment reinforces positive behaviour and encourages continued commitment to safety. This recognition can take various forms, such as verbal praise, safety awards, or team celebrations for achieving safety milestones. Celebrating safety successes not only boosts morale but also instills a sense of pride in maintaining a safe workplace. Employee involvement in safety decision-making processes significantly impacts their attitude. When employees have opportunities to contribute to safety discussions, policies, and initiatives, they feel a sense of ownership and responsibility.

Engaging employees in safety committees or soliciting their feedback empowers them to share concerns and suggestions, fostering a culture of collaboration and mutual respect. Employees' attitudes towards safety in industries are shaped by various factors, including organizational culture, management commitment, training, peer influence, recognition, and involvement in safety processes. Cultivating positive attitude towards safety is essential for creating a proactive safety culture, enhancing compliance, and reducing workplace incidents.

CHAPTER SIX

INTEGRATING SAFETY INTO DAILY LIFE ROUTINE

Creating a safety-first mindset is essential for fostering a culture where safety is prioritized in every aspect of life, both at work and at home. This mindset begins with awareness. Individuals must recognize that safety is not merely a set of rules to follow but a fundamental part of daily decision-making and behaviour.

The first step in cultivating this mindset is education. Providing comprehensive training on safety procedures, potential hazards, and risk management empowers individuals to understand the importance of safety measures. When people are well-informed, they are more likely to take safety seriously and make it a priority in their daily routines. Encouraging open communication is another critical element in creating a safety-first mindset. Organizations should promote an environment where individuals feel comfortable discussing safety concerns and suggesting improvements without fear of reprisal. Regular safety meetings or informal discussions can help keep safety at the forefront of everyone's mind, allowing team members to share experiences and learn from one another.

Integrating safety reminders into daily practices can reinforce this mindset. Visual cues, such as safety posters, checklists, or even smartphone alerts, can serve as constant reminders of the importance of safety in various tasks. These reminders help keep safety top of mind, especially in high-paced or distracting environments. Another effective strategy is to lead by example.

At home, parents and elders should model safe behaviour in their actions, demonstrating a commitment to safety that others can emulate. Acknowledging individuals or teams for their commitment to safety not only reinforces positive behaviour but also motivates others to prioritize safety. Fostering a sense of personal accountability is crucial for developing a safety-first mindset. Individuals should understand that they are responsible for their own safety as well as the safety of their colleagues and family members. Encouraging family members to look out for one another promotes a culture of shared responsibility, where everyone feels empowered to speak up about unsafe conditions or behaviour.

Incorporating safety into daily routines can further strengthen this mindset. Simple practices, such as conducting safety checks before starting a task or taking a moment to assess potential hazards in the environment, can become ingrained habits that promote a safety-first approach. Stress, fatigue, and distractions can significantly impact decision-making, so promoting practices like stress management and regular breaks is beneficial. Regularly reviewing safety practices and outcomes allows individuals to identify areas for improvement and reinforces the commitment to safety.

Put Safety in Gear: Drive with Care! - Safe driving habits are crucial for ensuring the safety of not just the driver but also passengers and other road users. Incorporating practices such as wearing seatbelts, avoiding distractions, and adhering to traffic rules into your daily commute can significantly reduce the risk of accidents and create a more secure driving environment.

One of the simplest yet most effective safety measures is the consistent use of seatbelts. Regardless of the distance being travelled, all occupants of a vehicle should buckle up before the car starts moving. Seatbelts are proven to save lives and reduce the severity of injuries in the event of a collision. Making it a habit to check that everyone is secured before driving sets a positive example and reinforces the importance of this basic safety measure.

Equally important is the need to avoid distractions while driving. In today's fast-paced world, distractions come in many forms, including mobile phones, navigation systems, and even conversations with passengers. To promote safe driving habits, it is essential to establish a no-phone policy while driving. This includes not only texting or calling but also browsing social media or checking notifications. Before starting the commute, drivers should ensure that their GPS is set up and that they have a clear plan for the route.

Using hands-free devices can minimize distractions, but the best practice is to focus solely on driving. Another critical aspect of safe driving is adhering to traffic rules and regulations. This includes obeying speed limits, stopping at red lights, yielding to pedestrians, and using turn signals when changing lanes or making turns. Understanding and respecting traffic signs helps maintain order on the road and prevents accidents caused by misunderstandings or miscommunications among drivers.

Incorporating defensive driving techniques can also enhance safety. This means being aware of your surroundings, anticipating the actions of other drivers, and being prepared to react appropriately. Keeping a safe following distance, using mirrors effectively, and staying vigilant can help prevent collisions, especially in high-traffic areas.

Weather conditions also play a significant role in safe driving. Adjusting driving habits according to the weather such as reducing speed during rain or snow can greatly increase safety. It is wise to ensure that your vehicle is in good condition, with regular maintenance checks for brakes, tires, and lights to avoid mechanical failures while on the road. Promoting safe driving habits extends beyond individual behaviour, it's also about fostering a culture of safety among family and friends. Encouraging loved ones to adopt similar habits, such as buckling up and avoiding distractions, creates a supportive environment where safety is a shared priority. For parents, Safe driving behaviour sets a powerful example for young passengers, instilling good habits that can last a lifetime.

Participating in driver safety courses can enhance knowledge and skills, offering valuable insights into safe driving techniques and the latest traffic regulations. These courses often emphasize the importance of continuous learning and self-awareness as a driver.

Hence, integrating safe driving habits into your daily commute is vital for reducing the risk of accidents and ensuring a safe environment for everyone on the road. By consistently wearing seatbelts, avoiding distractions, following traffic rules, and promoting a culture of safety, individuals can contribute to safer roads and set a positive example for others.

A Safe Home is a Happy Home! - Home safety is a critical aspect of creating a secure and comfortable living environment for you and your family. The home is where we should feel the safest, yet it can also present various risks if proper precautions are not taken.

To begin with, installing smoke detectors is essential, as they provide an early warning system in case of a fire. It is recommended to place detectors in every bedroom, hallway, and on each level of the home, ensuring they are tested at regular intervals. Carbon monoxide detectors are equally important, especially in homes with gas appliances or attached garages. These detectors should be placed near sleeping areas, and their healthiness should also be checked regularly.

In addition to fire safety measures, securing your home against break-ins is vital. This can be achieved by installing sturdy locks on all doors and windows, utilizing deadbolts, and considering a security system that includes cameras and alarms. The visibility of these security measures can often deter potential intruders. Furthermore, landscaping plays a role in home safety, keeping bushes trimmed and ensuring adequate outdoor lighting can eliminate hiding spots for potential burglars. Inside the home, it is crucial to create a safe environment for all family members, particularly children and elderly individuals. This can involve using safety gates to block stairways, securing heavy furniture to walls to prevent tipping, and ensuring that cleaning supplies and medications are stored out of reach.

It is also advisable to conduct regular safety checks to identify potential hazards, such as loose rugs that could cause tripping or wires that might pose a fire risk. Having an emergency plan in place is another essential component of home safety. This plan should include designated meeting spots outside the home, emergency contact information, and a list of essential supplies, such as first aid kits, flashlights, and non-perishable food items. Regularly practicing this plan with all family members ensures everyone knows what to do in case of an emergency.

Maintaining open lines of communication with neighbours can enhance community safety, getting to know your neighbours can foster a sense of vigilance and support in monitoring suspicious activities. If you are part of a community or homeowners' association, participating in neighbourhood watch programs can further strengthen local safety initiatives. It is also beneficial to educate family members about safety procedures, encouraging them to be aware of their surroundings and report any unusual activity.

When it comes to safety technology, utilizing smart home devices can provide added security and convenience. Smart doorbells, locks, and security cameras can be monitored remotely, allowing homeowners to keep an eye on their property even when they are away.

Establishing a fire escape plan that includes multiple routes out of the house can significantly enhance safety in the event of a fire. Practicing this escape plan and ensuring all family members are familiar with it will prepare everyone for quick action in an emergency. Finally, regularly reviewing and updating your safety measures is crucial, as circumstances and technologies change over time. By making home safety a priority, you can create a secure and nurturing environment that protects your loved ones and provides peace of mind. This proactive approach not only enhances your immediate safety but also fosters a greater sense of community well-being.

Prioritize Your Mental Well-Being! - Mental health is a vital aspect of overall well-being, influencing how we think, feel, and act in our daily lives. It encompasses a range of conditions that affect mood, thinking, and behaviour, including anxiety disorders, depression, and schizophrenia, among others. Maintaining good mental health is essential not only for personal happiness but also for productive interactions with others and the ability to handle the stresses of life.

One of the key components of mental health is emotional regulation, which allows individuals to manage their emotions effectively and respond to challenges with resilience. Poor mental health can lead to various consequences, such as decreased productivity, strained relationships, and physical health issues, illustrating the interconnectedness of mind and body. Recognizing the importance of mental health has led to increased awareness and a gradual reduction of the stigma associated with mental illness. This cultural shift encourages individuals to seek help without fear of judgement, promoting open conversations about mental health challenges and fostering supportive environments.

It is essential to understand that mental health issues can affect anyone, regardless of age, gender, or background, highlighting the need for comprehensive mental health education. Early intervention is crucial, as it can lead to better outcomes. Therefore, awareness of the signs and symptoms of mental health disorders is imperative. Symptoms such as persistent sadness, withdrawal from social activities, changes in appetite or sleep patterns, and difficulty concentrating can indicate underlying issues that warrant attention. Access to mental health resources, such as therapy, counseling, and support groups, plays a significant role in helping individuals navigate their struggles. Therapy, whether through cognitive-behavioural approaches, talk therapy, or other modalities, can provide valuable tools for coping with mental health challenges.

Mindfulness and relaxation techniques, such as meditation, yoga, and deep-breathing exercises, have also gained popularity as effective methods for enhancing mental well-being. Additionally, maintaining a healthy lifestyle contributes to mental health. Regular physical activity, a balanced diet, and adequate sleep are fundamental in promoting overall emotional wellness.

Social connections are equally important, as strong relationships can provide support, reduce feelings of isolation, and improve resilience against stress. Encouraging open dialogues within families, schools, and workplaces can foster understanding and empathy, creating a culture that prioritizes mental health. For workplaces, implementing mental health programs and promoting work-life balance can contribute to a healthier workforce, leading to improved productivity and morale. Schools play a crucial role as well, as integrating mental health education into curriculum can equip young people with coping strategies and resilience skills from an early age. Furthermore, leveraging technology through mental health apps and online resources has expanded access to support, especially for those who may feel uncomfortable seeking traditional forms of help.

As we continue to advance in our understanding of mental health, it is imperative to advocate for policies that promote mental health care access and prioritize research into effective treatments. The impact of the COVID-19 pandemic has emphasized the importance of mental health, as many individuals have faced increased levels of anxiety, depression, and uncertainty. As we move forward, fostering a culture that values mental health alongside physical health will be crucial in creating communities where individuals feel empowered to seek help, share their experiences, and support one another.

Your Health, Your Choice: Choose Wisely! - Incorporating regular exercise and balanced nutrition into daily life is essential for maintaining overall health and well-being. Both elements work synergistically to promote physical fitness, mental clarity, and emotional resilience. Regular exercise not only helps in managing weight but also enhances cardiovascular health, strengthens muscles and bones, and improves flexibility and balance. Engaging in physical activity releases endorphins, often referred to as "feel-good hormones," which can elevate mood and reduce feelings of stress and anxiety. This can be particularly beneficial in today's fast-paced world, where mental health challenges are increasingly prevalent.

To effectively incorporate exercise into a daily routine, it is recommended to find activities that you enjoy, whether it's dancing, swimming, cycling, or hiking. Setting realistic goals, such as aiming for at least 150 minutes of moderate-intensity aerobic activity each week, can help maintain motivation. Consistency is key, so scheduling workouts at specific times can turn exercise into a habitual part of your day, making it easier to stick with over time.

Incorporating strength training exercises at least thrice a week can improve muscle mass and metabolism, further enhancing physical health. On the other hand, balanced nutrition is equally crucial. A well-rounded diet includes a variety of fruits, vegetables, whole grains, lean proteins, and healthy fats, which provide the body with essential nutrients necessary for optimal functioning. Understanding portion sizes and being mindful of food choices can prevent overeating and promote better energy levels throughout the day.

It is important to limit processed foods, excessive sugars, and saturated fats, which can contribute to a range of health issues, including obesity, diabetes, and heart disease. Meal planning can be a helpful strategy, allowing individuals to prepare healthy meals in advance and make better food choices, even on busy days. Cooking at home not only promotes healthier eating habits but also encourages creativity and mindfulness around food. Staying hydrated is an often-overlooked aspect of nutrition. Drinking plenty of water throughout the day supports metabolism, digestion, and overall bodily functions. The relationship between nutrition and exercise cannot be overstated. The body requires proper fuel to perform optimally during physical activity. Consuming a balanced meal or snack that includes carbohydrates, proteins, and healthy fats before and after workouts can enhance performance and aid in recovery. For example, a pre-workout snack like a banana with peanut butter provides quick energy, while a post-workout meal such as beans and vegetables help in muscle recovery.

Educating oneself about nutrition and exercise can empower individuals to make informed choices that align with their health goals. Community support can also play a significant role in maintaining these lifestyle changes. Joining a fitness class, participating in group workouts, or engaging in community-supported agriculture programs can foster accountability and motivation. Sharing experiences and challenges with others can create a sense of belonging and encouragement, making the journey toward better health more enjoyable.

By prioritizing physical activity and nourishing the body with wholesome foods, individuals can improve their quality of life, boost their energy levels, and enhance their overall mental and emotional well-being. Establishing these habits early on can lead to sustainable health practices that extend into later years, ensuring a vibrant and fulfilling life.

CHAPTER SEVEN

THE ROLE OF TECHNOLOGY IN ENHANCING SAFETY CULTURE

Stay Alert, Stay Safe: Monitor in Real-Time! - Real-time monitoring of safety conditions using technology has become a crucial element in enhancing workplace safety across various industries, fundamentally transforming how organizations manage risks and protect their employees. This approach harnesses advanced tools and systems to continuously track safety metrics, identify potential hazards, and facilitate immediate responses to dangerous situations. The necessity for real-time monitoring arises from the fast-paced and often unpredictable nature of modern work environments, where traditional safety practices, such as periodic inspections and reactive measures, may not adequately address the evolving risks workers face daily.

By implementing real-time monitoring technologies, organizations can shift from a reactive to a proactive safety culture, significantly reducing the likelihood of accidents and injuries. One of the most prominent technologies facilitating real-time monitoring is the Internet of Things (IoT), which encompasses a network of interconnected devices equipped with sensors that can collect and transmit data about environmental conditions. For instance, IoT sensors can monitor air quality, temperature, humidity, and the presence of hazardous materials, providing organizations with constant visibility into safety conditions. When these sensors detect anomalies such as gas leaks or unsafe temperature levels they can trigger immediate alerts to relevant persons, allowing for quick intervention and minimizing the risk of accidents. This quick action not only enhances safety but also fosters a culture of accountability, as employees feel empowered to act upon real-time data.

Wearable technology has also revolutionized real-time safety monitoring. Devices such as smart helmets, vests, and wristbands can track workers' vital signs, movements, and exposure to environmental hazards. For example, a wearable device may monitor a worker's heart rate, fatigue levels, and location, providing alerts when thresholds are exceeded or when workers enter hazardous areas. This capability not only protects individual workers but also signals to the entire workforce that their health and safety are prioritized. Wearable technology can provide data for continuous improvement, allowing organizations to analyse patterns in worker behaviour and health metrics to develop better safety procedures. Video surveillance systems, particularly those equipped with advanced analytics, play a vital role in monitoring safety conditions in real-time.

Closed-circuit television (CCTV) cameras can now be integrated with artificial intelligence to analyse video feeds for unsafe behaviour or condition. For instance, AI can identify when employees are not wearing personal protective equipment (PPE) or entering restricted areas, sending immediate alerts to supervisors. This capability ensures that safety procedures are consistently enforced and provides a level of oversight that is difficult to achieve with manual monitoring alone.

Drones are another innovative tool for real-time safety monitoring, particularly in industries such as construction, agriculture, and emergency response. Drones can provide aerial views of work sites, allowing for the inspection of hard-to-reach areas and the identification of safety hazards from a unique perspective. Equipped with cameras and sensors, drones can conduct routine inspections and monitor compliance with safety regulations, thus enhancing situational awareness for safety managers. The integration of these technologies offers a range of benefits that contribute to a safer work environment.

Real-time monitoring enhances situational awareness by providing organizations with a comprehensive understanding of safety conditions at any given moment. By visualizing data through dashboards and analytics tools, safety managers can quickly assess risks, prioritize interventions, and allocate resources effectively. This enhanced situational awareness fosters a proactive approach to safety, where potential issues are addressed before they escalate into serious problems.

Compliance with safety regulations is another critical benefit of real-time monitoring. Automated data collection ensures that safety records are accurate and up-to-date, simplifying the process of demonstrating compliance during audits. Real-time reporting capabilities allow organizations to track safety performance metrics, identify trends, and implement corrective actions promptly. By maintaining rigorous compliance with safety standards, organizations reinforce a culture of accountability and demonstrate their commitment to worker well-being. Despite the numerous advantages, organizations must also navigate certain challenges when implementing real-time monitoring systems.

One significant hurdle is the integration of these technologies with existing safety management systems. Organizations must ensure that new tools and technologies can seamlessly communicate with legacy systems to provide a cohesive overview of safety conditions. This may require investments in additional software or hardware and thoughtful planning to avoid disruptions during the transition.

Another challenge relates to data privacy and security. As organizations collect and transmit vast amounts of safety-related data, concerns about data protection become paramount. Implementing robust cybersecurity measures is essential to safeguarding sensitive information from breaches or unauthorized access. Organizations should establish clear policies regarding data usage and employee privacy to build trust and transparency among the workforce. Employee training and acceptance are also critical to the successful implementation of real-time monitoring technologies.

Organizations must invest in comprehensive training programs that familiarize employees with new tools and technologies, emphasizing the benefits for their safety and well-being. Building trust and transparency around the use of monitoring technologies is essential to encourage buy-in from the workforce, ensuring that employees feel comfortable and secure in their work environment. Looking to the future, several trends are emerging in the realm of real-time monitoring that will further enhance safety conditions in the workplace. The integration of artificial intelligence (AI) and machine learning (ML) into real-time monitoring systems is poised to elevate predictive capabilities significantly. These technologies can analyse historical data to identify patterns and predict potential safety incidents, allowing organizations to take preventive measures before issues arise.

The growing prevalence of cloud-based solutions is transforming how organizations access and manage safety data. Cloud platforms enable real-time data access from anywhere, facilitating collaboration among safety teams and enhancing data sharing across departments. This flexibility promotes a holistic approach to safety management, ensuring that all stakeholders are informed and engaged in safety practices. The evolution of wearable technology is expected to continue, with new devices likely to emerge featuring advanced functionalities such as environmental sensing. These innovations will provide even greater insights into worker safety and health, reinforcing the importance of individual well-being in a safety-oriented culture. As technology continues to evolve, organizations that embrace real-time monitoring will be better equipped to protect their workforce, create a safer operational environment.

Transforming Safety with Smart Data Insights! - Data analytics tools play a pivotal role in analysing safety-related data to identify trends and patterns that can significantly enhance workplace safety and operational efficiency. In an era where organizations are submerged with vast amounts of data, the ability to transform raw information into actionable insights is crucial for fostering a proactive safety culture. By leveraging sophisticated data analytics techniques, companies can not only understand historical safety incidents but also predict potential risks, allowing them to take preventive measures before accidents occur.

At the core of this process is the collection of safety-related data, which can include incident reports, near-misses, safety audits, equipment maintenance, and environmental conditions. By aggregating this data from various sources, organizations create a comprehensive database that serves as the foundation for analysis. Data analytics tools, such as statistical software, machine learning algorithms, and visualization platforms, enable organizations to process and interpret this information effectively.

One of the primary advantages of using data analytics in safety management is the ability to identify trends over time. For instance, by analysing incident reports over several years, organizations can recognize patterns that might not be immediately obvious. They may find that certain types of incidents occur more frequently during specific times of the year, or that particular departments are more prone to accidents. Identifying these trends allows organizations to implement targeted interventions, such as enhanced training programs for high risk areas.

Advanced analytics can help organizations identify root causes of incidents. Traditional safety analyses often focus on the surface-level factors of an accident, such as the actions taken by individuals involved. However, data analytics tools can dig deeper, revealing underlying systemic issues that contribute to unsafe conditions. For example, by analysing equipment failure data alongside incident reports, organizations may discover that certain machinery is more prone to malfunctions in specific environmental conditions. Understanding these relationships allows organizations to address the root causes of safety incidents, rather than merely treating the symptoms.

Machine learning algorithms are particularly valuable in this context, as they can process large datasets and uncover correlations that human analysts might overlook. Predictive analytics is another powerful application of data analytics in safety management. By utilizing historical data to forecast future incidents, organizations can take a proactive stance in their safety initiatives. For example, if data analytics reveals a correlation between certain operational practices and an increase in near-misses, organizations can adjust their processes before a more serious incident occurs. Predictive models can also account for various external factors, such as weather conditions, further enhancing the accuracy of risk assessments.

Visualization tools play a critical role in communicating safety data effectively to stakeholders at all levels of an organization. Dashboards and interactive reports can display key performance indicators (KPIs), incident trends, and risk assessments in a visually engaging format. By presenting data in a way that is easy to understand, organizations can foster a culture of safety awareness among employees. When workers can visualize trends in safety incidents, they are more likely to recognize the importance of adhering to safety procedures and participating in safety initiatives.

Data analytics tools can facilitate benchmarking against industry standards or similar organizations. By comparing their safety performance metrics with those of others, organizations can identify areas for improvement and set realistic safety goals. This benchmarking process can motivate teams to strive for excellence, as they aim to meet or exceed industry standards.

Organizations can utilize analytics to assess the effectiveness of safety training programs and initiatives. By analysing incident data before and after training sessions, organizations can measure changes in safety performance and determine whether specific interventions are yielding positive results. This feedback loop enables continuous improvement in safety practices and ensures that training efforts are aligned with organizational goals. However, to fully harness the power of data analytics in safety management, organizations must address several challenges.

One significant hurdle is ensuring data quality and consistency. Inconsistent data entry practices or incomplete records can lead to misleading conclusions, undermining the effectiveness of analyses. Organizations must establish clear procedures for data collection and entry, ensuring that all relevant information is captured accurately. Fostering a culture of data-driven decision-making is essential. Employees at all levels must understand the importance of data analytics in safety management and feel empowered to utilize the tools available to them. This may involve training sessions to familiarize employees with analytics tools and emphasizing the role of data in identifying and mitigating safety risks.

As organizations embrace digital transformation, integrating data analytics tools with existing safety management systems can enhance their effectiveness. This integration allows for seamless data flow, enabling real-time analysis and reporting. By combining data from various sources, organizations can gain a holistic view of safety performance and make informed decisions based on comprehensive insights. As industries continue to evolve and face new challenges, the role of data analytics in safety management will only become more critical, enabling organizations to adapt, innovate, and thrive in an increasingly complex landscape.

Train Smarter: Dive into VR and AR for Ultimate Safety! - Virtual reality (VR) and Augmented reality (AR) have emerged as transformative technologies in the field of safety training, revolutionizing how organizations educate and prepare their workforce for potential hazards and emergency situations. These immersive technologies create highly engaging and interactive learning environments that enhance knowledge retention, improve skills acquisition, and ultimately contribute to a safer workplace.

One of the most significant advantages of using VR and AR in safety training is their ability to simulate real-world scenarios without the associated risks. In traditional training methods, employees often learn through lectures, videos, or static demonstrations, which may not adequately prepare them for the dynamic nature of real-life situations. VR technology, on the other hand, immerses trainees in a three-dimensional environment where they can practice their responses to various safety scenarios, such as fire evacuations, equipment malfunctions, or hazardous material spills. This experiential learning approach allows participants to engage with their surroundings and make decisions in real time, which fosters a deeper understanding of the procedures necessary for maintaining safety. In a VR training environment, learners can encounter realistic challenges that replicate their actual job conditions, enabling them to develop critical problem-solving skills and situational awareness. For instance, a construction worker can experience a virtual job site where they must navigate potential hazards, such as falling objects or unsafe scaffolding, learning to identify risks and respond appropriately. This hands-on experience builds confidence and competence, allowing employees to practice their skills repeatedly without the fear of real-world consequences.

VR and AR can provide immediate feedback on trainees' performance, further enhancing the learning experience. As participants engage with the training modules, the system can track their actions and decisions, offering real-time assessments and guidance. This instant feedback loop allows trainees to recognize mistakes and adjust their approaches, promoting continuous improvement in their safety practices. The ability to simulate various scenarios also means that training can be designed to specific roles within an organization, ensuring that employees receive relevant instruction that aligns with their job responsibilities. AR complements VR by overlaying digital information onto the physical world, providing valuable context and guidance during safety training. For example, AR can enhance on-the-job training by offering real-time instructions or safety reminders as employees navigate their work environment. When workers wear AR glasses, they can see visual cues, such as warning signs, superimposed onto their field of view, helping them stay aware of potential hazards. This integration of digital information not only reinforces training but also serves as a constant reminder of safety best practices, contributing to a culture of safety within the organization.

Another notable benefit of VR and AR in safety training is their ability to facilitate remote learning and collaboration. In today's increasingly global workforce, organizations often have employees located in various regions, making it challenging to provide consistent safety training across all locations. VR and AR can bridge this gap by offering virtual training sessions that can be accessed from anywhere, allowing employees to participate in safety drills and exercises regardless of their physical location. This flexibility not only saves time and resources but also ensures that all employees receive standardized training, reducing the risk of knowledge gaps.

The immersive nature of VR and AR training can lead to higher levels of engagement and motivation among participants. Traditional training methods often struggle to capture learners' attention, resulting in passive participation and limited retention of information. In contrast, VR and AR provide an interactive and visually stimulating experience that keeps trainees engaged and invested in their learning. By immersing learners in a captivating environment, these technologies help foster a sense of ownership over their training, encouraging them to take safety seriously and apply their knowledge in real-world situations. Beyond immediate training applications, VR and AR can also play a role in ongoing safety assessments and evaluations. Organizations can utilize these technologies to conduct regular safety drills and exercises, allowing employees to maintain their skills and stay prepared for emergencies. For instance, companies can simulate disaster scenarios, such as earthquakes or chemical spills, enabling teams to practice their response plans and assess their effectiveness. By incorporating VR and AR into regular training regimens, organizations can create a culture of continuous learning and improvement, ensuring that safety remains a top priority.

While the benefits of VR and AR in safety training are substantial, organizations must also consider certain challenges associated with implementation. One challenge is the initial investment required to develop and deploy these technologies. Creating high-quality VR and AR training modules can involve significant costs, including the purchase of hardware, software development, and content creation. However, many organizations find that the long-term benefits of reduced accidents, improved employee performance, and enhanced safety culture far outweigh the upfront costs.

Organizations must ensure that employees are adequately trained to use VR and AR systems effectively. This may involve providing orientation sessions and ongoing support to help workers navigate the technology and maximize its benefits. By fostering a culture of innovation and adaptability, organizations can encourage employees to embrace these new training methods and integrate them into their professional development.

Another consideration is the need for content that accurately reflects real-world conditions and scenarios. Training modules must be carefully designed to provide realistic experiences that align with the specific risks and challenges employees face in their roles. Collaboration with subject matter experts and safety professionals can help organizations develop effective training content that meets industry standards and addresses relevant safety concerns.

Spot It, Snap It, Send It: Safety Made Simple! - Mobile applications designed for reporting safety hazards and incidents have emerged as powerful tools for enhancing workplace safety and fostering a culture of proactive risk management. In an era where smartphones are found everywhere, these dedicated apps empower employees to report safety concerns swiftly and efficiently, ensuring that potential risks are addressed before they escalate into serious incidents. The significance of mobile reporting apps lies in their ability to provide a streamlined, user-friendly platform for employees to communicate safety issues in real time.

Traditional methods of hazard reporting, such as paper forms or verbal notifications, can be cumbersome, leading to delays in addressing safety concerns. In contrast, mobile applications allow workers to report hazards instantly, often with just a few taps on their devices. This immediacy is crucial in high-risk environments, where timely interventions can prevent accidents and protect employee well-being.

One of the standout features of these apps is their ease of use. Most mobile reporting applications are designed with intuitive interfaces that guide users through the reporting process. Employees can easily select the type of hazard they are encountering, add descriptions, and attach images or videos to provide context. This visual documentation enhances the clarity of reports, making it easier for safety officers to assess and address the issues. By simplifying the reporting process, mobile apps encourage more employees to participate in hazard reporting, thereby fostering a culture of shared responsibility for safety within the organization.

These applications often come equipped with geolocation features that automatically tag the location of the reported hazard. This capability is particularly beneficial in large facilities or outdoor environments where hazards may not be easily identifiable. By pinpointing the exact location of an issue, safety teams can respond more efficiently, reducing the time it takes to resolve safety concerns. Geolocation data can be invaluable for identifying patterns or trends in safety incidents across various areas of a facility, allowing organizations to implement targeted safety measures. The integration of mobile apps with existing safety management systems further enhances their effectiveness.

Many organizations utilize comprehensive safety management software to track incidents, conduct audits, and manage compliance. By connecting mobile reporting apps to these systems, organizations can ensure that all reported hazards are logged and monitored in real time. This integration allows for seamless data collection and analysis, enabling safety managers to identify trends and make data-driven decisions about safety improvements. For example, if multiple employees report similar hazards in a particular area, safety managers can investigate the root causes and implement corrective actions to mitigate risks.

Another key advantage of mobile applications for reporting safety hazards is their potential to promote employee engagement in safety initiatives. By empowering workers to share their concerns, organizations can create a more inclusive safety culture where employees feel valued and heard. This sense of ownership encourages individuals to take an active role in promoting safety, leading to greater overall awareness and vigilance.

Many apps also feature functionalities that allow employees to receive feedback on their reports, fostering a sense of accountability and collaboration between staff and safety teams. Beyond incident reporting, these applications can also serve as platforms for sharing safety resources and best practices. Mobile applications for reporting hazards can also play a crucial role in crisis management and emergency response. In situations where immediate action is required such as during a fire or chemical spill, apps can facilitate rapid communication between employees and emergency response teams. By providing a dedicated channel for reporting emergencies, organizations can streamline their response efforts, ensuring that help arrives promptly and efficiently. These applications can include features such as emergency contact lists, evacuation maps, and real-time alerts, equipping employees with the information they need to respond effectively in critical situations. While the benefits of mobile apps for reporting safety hazards are substantial, organizations must also consider several challenges associated with their implementation.

One primary concern is ensuring that all employees are comfortable using the technology. Training sessions may be necessary to familiarize staff with the app's features and functionality, particularly for those who may be less tech-savvy. Organizations should prioritize user-friendly designs and provide ongoing support to address any technical issues that may arise.

Data privacy and security are also critical considerations when implementing mobile reporting apps. Organizations must ensure that reported information is handled with confidentiality and that employees feel secure in their reporting. Clear policies regarding data usage and protection should be communicated to all users to build trust in the reporting system. Organizations should implement robust security measures to safeguard sensitive information from unauthorized access or breaches.

To maximize the effectiveness of mobile applications for reporting safety hazards, organizations should also promote a culture of open communication around safety concerns. Encouraging employees to report issues without fear of retaliation is essential for fostering a proactive safety environment. Leadership should emphasize the importance of hazard reporting and recognize individuals who contribute to safety improvements, reinforcing the idea that everyone plays a role in maintaining a safe workplace.

Continuous evaluation and improvement of the mobile reporting system are crucial for its long-term success. Organizations should regularly solicit feedback from users to identify areas for enhancement and ensure that the app continues to meet the needs of employees.

Wear the Future: Smart Gear for Safer Work! - Wearable devices, such as smart helmets and safety vests equipped with sensors, are revolutionizing workplace safety and health monitoring by providing real-time data that enhances the protection of workers across various industries. These innovative technologies are designed to track vital health metrics, environmental conditions, and safety compliance, allowing organizations to proactively address potential risks and ensure the well-being of their employees.

One of the most significant advantages of wearable devices is their ability to continuously monitor the physiological parameters of workers. Smart helmets can be equipped with sensors that track heart rate, body temperature, and even fatigue levels. By collecting this data, organizations can identify signs of overexertion or heat stress before they lead to serious health issues. For example, if a worker's heart rate exceeds a certain threshold or if their body temperature rises dangerously high, the helmet can alert both the worker and their supervisors, prompting immediate action to prevent heat-related illnesses or cardiovascular issues. This proactive monitoring not only protects individual workers but also contributes to overall workplace safety by reducing the likelihood of accidents related to health crises.

In addition to health monitoring, wearable devices can provide crucial information about environmental conditions. Smart safety vests can include sensors that detect exposure to hazardous substances, such as toxic gases or chemicals, and alert workers to potential dangers. These devices can also monitor factors like noise levels and air quality, helping organizations ensure compliance with occupational health and safety regulations. For instance, if a worker enters an area with high noise levels, the vest can vibrate to remind them to wear appropriate hearing protection. This real-time feedback empowers workers to make informed decisions about their safety, creating a more vigilant and responsive workforce.

Another key feature of smart helmets and safety vests is their ability to facilitate communication and collaboration among team members. Many of these devices are equipped with built-in communication systems that allow workers to communicate with each other and with safety officers without having to remove their helmets or vests. This hands-free communication is particularly beneficial in noisy or hazardous environments, where verbal communication can be challenging. For example, in construction sites or factories, workers can instantly report safety concerns or request assistance while remaining focused on their tasks. This immediate communication helps create a culture of safety awareness, where employees feel empowered to address potential hazards as they arise.

Additionally, wearable devices can assist in location tracking, providing organizations with valuable insights into workers' movements throughout job sites. By utilizing GPS and other location-tracking technologies, companies can ensure that workers are in safe areas and can quickly locate individuals in case of emergencies. This capability is particularly critical in high-risk industries, such as construction, mining, and oil and gas, where workers may operate in remote or hazardous locations. If an emergency occurs, supervisors can use real-time location data to coordinate rescue efforts efficiently, potentially saving lives and reducing the impact of incidents.

The integration of wearable devices into workplace safety programs also aligns with the growing trend of data-driven decision-making. Organizations can collect and analyse data from these devices to identify patterns and trends in worker health and safety. For example, by examining data related to fatigue levels, organizations can implement strategies to manage workloads and reduce the risk of accidents caused by tiredness. Similarly, data on exposure to hazardous substances can inform safety training programs and highlight areas that require additional protective measures. This continuous improvement cycle not only enhances workplace safety but also fosters a culture of accountability and responsibility among employees. While the benefits of wearable devices in monitoring workers' health and safety are substantial, organizations must also address potential challenges associated with their implementation. One significant consideration is the need for employee's acceptance of the technology.

Some workers may have concerns about privacy or feel that constant monitoring infringes on their personal space. To mitigate these concerns, organizations should prioritize transparent communication about the purpose of wearable devices and how the data will be used. Involving employees in the decision-making process and providing training on the technology can also help build trust and ensure that workers understand the benefits of real-time monitoring for their safety and well-being.

Data security and privacy are also critical considerations when implementing wearable devices. Organizations must establish robust procedures to protect sensitive health and location data from unauthorized access or breaches. This may involve encrypting data, limiting access to authorized persons, and regularly updating security measures to address potential vulnerabilities. Ensuring that employees are informed about data privacy policies can further enhance trust in the system and encourage participation in health and safety monitoring initiatives.

Another consideration is the need for reliable connectivity, as wearable devices often rely on network access to transmit data in real-time. In remote or isolated work environments, maintaining a stable internet connection can be challenging. Organizations should assess the connectivity needs of their workforce and consider implementing solutions, such as mesh networks or satellite connections, to ensure that data is consistently transmitted and monitored.

The effectiveness of wearable devices in enhancing workplace safety also depends on the quality and accuracy of the sensors used. Organizations must invest in high-quality technology that provides reliable readings and minimizes false alarms. Regular maintenance and calibration of devices are essential to ensure their ongoing functionality and effectiveness in monitoring health and safety conditions.

As industries continue to evolve and prioritize employee well-being, the integration of wearable devices will play a crucial role in creating safer work environments and fostering a culture of continuous improvement in health and safety practices.

Proactive Safety: Your Digital Partner in Incident Management! - Digital tools have become essential in modern incident management, providing organizations with the capability to document incidents, analyse root causes, and develop corrective actions effectively. These tools streamline the process of incident reporting and investigation, transforming the way organizations approach safety and risk management.

One of the primary advantages of digital incident management tools is their ability to facilitate immediate and comprehensive documentation. Traditional methods of incident reporting often rely on paper forms or spreadsheets, which can be prone to errors, and difficult to track over time. In contrast, digital tools enable employees to report incidents instantly through user-friendly interfaces on smartphones, tablets, or computers. These platforms often allow users to input key details such as the nature of the incident, the location, the individuals involved, and any contributing factors.

Many tools also include functionalities for attaching photos, videos, or audio recordings, which provide valuable context and enhance the clarity of reports. This comprehensive documentation is crucial for establishing an accurate account of incidents, enabling organizations to conduct thorough investigations and gather critical data for analysis. Furthermore, digital tools streamline the incident reporting process by enabling automated workflows that ensure timely follow-up and accountability. When an incident is reported, the system can automatically notify relevant stakeholders, such as safety managers, supervisors, or compliance officers, ensuring that the right people are informed promptly. This automation reduces the risk of delays in response and encourages a culture of accountability, as employees can easily see the status of their reports and any actions taken in response.

Digital tools often feature customizable dashboards and reporting functionalities that allow organizations to analyse incident data effectively. By aggregating and visualizing incident reports, these platforms help identify trends, patterns, and recurring issues that may require attention. For example, if an organization notices a spike in slips and falls during certain times of the year or in specific locations, this data can prompt a deeper investigation into environmental factors, employee behaviour, or training needs. The ability to analyse data in real time empowers organizations to make informed decisions about safety improvements and allocate resources effectively.

A critical component of incident management is the root cause analysis, which seeks to identify the underlying factors that contribute to incidents. Digital tools often incorporate root cause analysis methodologies, allowing organizations to systematically investigate incidents and determine their root causes. Techniques such as the "5 Whys," Fishbone diagrams, and Fault Tree Analysis can be integrated into the software, guiding users through the process of identifying contributing factors and establishing causal relationships. By leveraging these methodologies, organizations can move beyond superficial solutions and address the fundamental issues that lead to incidents, ultimately improving overall safety performance.

Digital tools enhance collaboration among stakeholders involved in the incident investigation process. Many platforms include features for assigning tasks, sharing documents, and providing feedback, fostering a collaborative approach to safety management. When employees, supervisors, and safety officers, work together to investigate incidents, they can leverage diverse perspectives and expertise to uncover root causes and develop effective corrective actions. This collaborative effort not only strengthens the quality of the analysis but also encourages a sense of ownership and engagement in the safety process. Once root causes have been identified, digital tools play a crucial role in developing and tracking corrective actions.

Organizations can create action plans within the software, assigning responsibilities and deadlines to ensure accountability. The ability to monitor the status of corrective actions in real time helps organizations stay on track and ensure that identified issues are addressed promptly.

Many digital tools offer features for tracking the effectiveness of implemented corrective actions over time. By measuring key performance indicators (KPIs) and conducting follow-up assessments, organizations can evaluate whether their interventions have successfully reduced incidents or improved safety conditions. This continuous feedback loop is essential for fostering a culture of continuous improvement, where organizations learn from incidents and adapt their practices accordingly.

Another significant benefit of digital tools in incident management is their ability to facilitate compliance with regulatory requirements. Many industries are subject to stringent safety regulations and standards that require detailed documentation and reporting of incidents. Digital incident management tools can automate the reporting process, ensuring that organizations meet their legal obligations while reducing the administrative burden on safety officer. By maintaining accurate and easily accessible records, organizations can demonstrate compliance during audits and inspections, minimizing the risk of penalties or legal issues. Furthermore, the integration of digital tools with other safety management systems can enhance the overall effectiveness of incident reporting and analysis. For example, organizations can link incident data with training management systems to identify gaps in employee training related to specific incidents.

By analysing the relationship between incidents and training records, organizations can develop targeted training programs that address identified risks and improve employee preparedness. Similarly, integrating incident management tools with equipment maintenance systems can help organizations identify trends related to equipment failures and establish preventive maintenance procedures. While the benefits of digital tools for incident documentation, analysis, and corrective action development are substantial, organizations must also consider several challenges associated with their implementation.

One of the primary concerns is ensuring user adoption and engagement with the technology. Employees may be resistant to change, particularly if they are accustomed to traditional reporting methods. To overcome this hurdle, organizations should provide comprehensive training and support to familiarize employees with the digital tools and highlight the benefits of using them for incident reporting and safety improvement. Building a culture that values data-driven decision-making and emphasizes the importance of incident reporting is essential for fostering engagement.

Data security and privacy are also critical considerations when implementing digital incident management tools. Organizations must ensure that sensitive incident data is protected from unauthorized access and breaches. Organizations should also continuously evaluate and improve their incident management processes and digital tools. Regularly soliciting feedback from users can help identify areas for enhancement and ensure that the tools remain effective and user-friendly.

Compliance Made Easy: Empowering Safety with Technology! - Using technology to maintain compliance with safety regulations and standards has become a fundamental aspect of modern workplace safety management. In an increasingly complex regulatory landscape, organizations are turning to digital solutions to streamline compliance processes, improve tracking and reporting, and ensure that safety standards are met consistently.

One of the most significant advantages of leveraging technology for compliance is the automation of documentation and reporting. Traditional compliance methods often involve manual record-keeping, which can be labour-intensive and prone to errors. Digital tools, such as compliance management software, allow organizations to automate the collection and management of safety-related data. These tools can generate reports that align with regulatory requirements, ensuring that all necessary information is readily available for audits and inspections. By automating these processes, organizations can reduce the risk of non-compliance due to oversight or incomplete records, allowing safety officers to focus on proactive measures rather than administrative tasks.

Technology enables organizations to maintain real-time visibility into their compliance status. Many compliance management systems feature dashboards that provide a comprehensive overview of safety performance, including key performance indicators (KPIs), incident reports, and audit results. This visibility allows safety managers to identify trends and potential areas of concern quickly, facilitating timely interventions. For example, if an organization notices an increase in incident reports in a specific department, it can trigger a review of safety practices and compliance with regulations in that area. This proactive approach to compliance not only helps mitigate risks but also fosters a culture of accountability within the organization.

Technology can enhance communication and collaboration among team members involved in compliance efforts. Many compliance management platforms include features that allow for task assignment, document sharing, and real-time updates, ensuring that everyone is aligned and informed about compliance-related activities. For instance, safety managers can assign specific compliance tasks to team members, such as conducting safety inspections or completing training modules, and monitor progress through the platform. This collaborative approach streamlines compliance efforts and ensures that all team members understand their roles in maintaining safety standards.

Training and education are critical components of compliance, and technology can play a significant role in enhancing these initiatives. E-learning platforms and training management systems allow organizations to deliver safety training and compliance courses efficiently. These tools can track employee progress and completion rates, ensuring that all personnel are up-to-date on the latest safety regulations and practices. Technology can facilitate the development of training programs that address specific compliance requirements relevant to different departments or job roles. For example, a manufacturing facility may implement specialized training modules for employees working with hazardous materials, ensuring that they are well-versed in the applicable regulations and safety procedures.

Another significant aspect of using technology for compliance is the ability to conduct audits and inspections more efficiently. Digital tools can streamline the audit process by providing checklists and templates that align with regulatory requirements. Safety officers can complete inspections using mobile devices, allowing for immediate documentation of findings and issues. Many platforms also allow for the attachment of photos and comments, providing valuable context for audit results. This immediacy not only enhances the accuracy of audit reports but also enables organizations to take corrective actions quickly when compliance gaps are identified. In the context of regulatory changes, technology can help organizations stay informed and adapt to evolving compliance requirements.

Technology can facilitate the integration of compliance efforts with broader risk management initiatives. Many organizations are adopting holistic approaches to safety that encompass not only regulatory compliance but also overall risk mitigation. By integrating compliance management systems with risk assessment tools, organizations can identify potential hazards and compliance gaps simultaneously. This comprehensive view allows for more informed decision-making regarding resource allocation and safety priorities.

Conclusion - Nurturing A Sustainable Safety Culture

As we conclude this exploration of building a safety culture within organizations, it is essential to reflect on the journey we have taken together. A strong safety culture is not merely a set of policies or compliance checklists. It is a living, breathing aspect of an organization that shapes behaviour, attitude, and ultimately, outcomes. It requires the collective commitment of everyone from leadership to employees to prioritize safety as a core value rather than a mere obligation.

Throughout this book, we have discussed the critical components necessary for fostering a safety culture - leadership commitment, employee engagement, positive mindset, honest communication, continuous improvement, and the importance of feedback mechanisms. These elements are interconnected, creating a framework where safety can flourish. Remember, a safety culture is built over time, nurtured through ongoing effort and unwavering dedication.

It is important to understand that the journey toward a robust safety culture is continuous. There will always be new challenges and evolving risks, but with a solid foundation in safety principles, organizations can navigate these changes effectively. Encourage a mindset of learning and adaptation. Celebrate successes and learn from failures. Every incident, near miss, and safety suggestion is an opportunity to enhance practices and reinforce the commitment to safety.

Your role is pivotal. Lead by example, promote transparency, and create an environment where every employee feels empowered to share their concerns and contribute to safety initiatives. Make safety an integral part of your organizational identity, where it is not just an afterthought but a fundamental aspect of how you operate.

In closing, commit to fostering a culture where safety is valued and prioritized. Engage with your teams, listen to their feedback, and be proactive in addressing safety concerns. Together, we can build not just safer workplaces but also a more resilient and engaged workforce. By investing in a culture of safety, we protect our most valuable asset—our people.

Disclaimer

The views in the book are entirely personal and do not reflect the opinion of author's employer.